THE UNSPEAKABLE ART OF BILL VIOLA

The
Unspeakable Art
of
Bill Viola

A Visual Theology

Ronald R. Bernier

PICKWICK *Publications* · Eugene, Oregon

THE UNSPEAKABLE ART OF BILL VIOLA
A Visual Theology

Pickwick Publications
An Imprint of Wipf and Stock Publishers
199 W. 8th Ave., Suite 3
Eugene, OR 97401

www.wipfandstock.com

ISBN 13: 978–1-62032–471-4

Cataloging-in-Publication data:

Bernier, Ronald R.

   The unspeakable art of Bill Viola : a visual theology / Ronald R. Bernier.

   xiv + 86 p. ; 23 cm. —Includes bibliographical references.

   ISBN 13: 978–1-62032–471-4

1. Viola, Bill, 1951–. 2. Art, Modern—20th century. 3. Spiritual life—Christianity. I. Title.

BV4501.3 .B47 2014

Manufactured in the U.S.A.

For Michael I. Podro, CBE, FBA
(1931–2008)

Contents

List of Illustrations | *ix*
Acknowledgments | *xiii*

1   Introduction: Towards a Visual Theology | 1

2   In the Dark Night of the Soul: *Room for St. John of the Cross* | 11

3   In Excess: Towards a Theological Sublime | 36

4   The Unseen Passions and the Ethics of Sublimity | 52

5   The Secret Tongue of the Heart: Some Final Remarks | 78

Bibliography | *83*

Illustrations

Figure 1: *Room for St. John of the Cross*, 1983 | 12

Video/sound installation

14 x 24 x 30 ft. (4.3 x 7.3 x 9.1 m)

In a large dark room, and black cubicle with window, the illuminated interior containing peat moss on the floor, a wooden table, glass with water, metal pitcher with water, color video image on 3.7" monitor, one channel mono sound; black-and-white video projection on wall screen; amplified stereo sound.

Edition of two with one artist's proof.

Figure 2: detail | 12

Figures 3–5: *The Crossing*, 1996 | 54, 55

Video/sound installation

490 x 840 x 1740 cm

Two channels of color video projections from opposite sides of large dark gallery onto two large back-to-back screens suspended from ceiling and mounted to floor; four channels of amplified stereo sound, four speakers.

Performer: Phil Esposito

Photo: Kira Perov

Figure 6: *Man of Sorrows*, 2001 | 56

Color video on freestanding LCD flat panel

19 3/8 x 15 x 6 in (49.2 x 38.1 x 15.2 cm)

Performer: John Fleck

16:00 minutes

Edition of five with one artist's proof

Figure 7: *Dolorosa*, 2000 | 57
Color video diptych on two freestanding hinged LCD flat panels
16 x 24 ½ x 5 ¾ in (40.6 x 62.2 x 14.6 cm)
Performers: Natasha Basley, Shishir Kurup
11:00 minutes
Edition of five with one artist's proof

Figure 8: Dieric Bouts, *Christ as Salvator Mundi*, c.1450 | 58
Museum Boijmans Van Beuningen, Rotterdam
Photographer: Studio Tromp, Rotterdam.

Figure 9: Workshop of Dieric Bouts, *Mater Dolorosa* (*Sorrowing Virgin*), 1480/1500, oil on panel, 38.7 x 30.3 cm (15 ¼ x 11 7/8 in.). | 59
Chester D. Tripp Fund; Chester D. Tripp Endowment; through prior acquisition of Max and Leola Epstein. 1986.998. The Art Institute of Chicago.

Figure 10: *The Quintet of the Astonished*, 2000 | 60
Color video rear projection on screen mounted on wall in dark room
Projected image size: 1.4 x 2.4 m; room dimensions variable
Performers: John Malpede, Weba Garretson, Tom Fitzpatrick, John Fleck, Dan Gerrity
15:20 minutes
Edition of three with one artist's proof

Figure 11: *The Quintet of Remembrance*, 2000 | 61
Color video rear projection on screen mounted on wall in dark room
Projected image size: 140 x 240 cm; room dimensions variable
Performers: Weba Garretson, John Malpede, Mary Pat Gleason, Valerie Spencer, Dan Gerrity
15:00 minutes
Edition of three with one artist's proof

Figure 12: *The Quintet of the Silent,* 2000 | 61

Color video on plasma display mounted on wall

28 ½ x 47 ½ x 4 in (72.4 x 120.7 x 10.2 cm)

Performers: Chris Grove, David Hernandez, John Malpede, Dan Gerrity, Tom Fitzpatrick

Edition of five with one artist's proof

16:26

Figure 13: *The Quintet of the Unseen,* 2000 | 62

Color video rear projection on screen mounted on wall in dark room

Projected image size: 140 x 240 cm; room dimensions variable

Performers: Valerie Spencer, Weba Garretson, John Malpede, John Fleck, Dan Gerrity

16:28 minutes

Edition of three with one artist's proof

Figure 14: Hieronymus Bosch, *Christ Mocked (The Crowning with Thorns)* c.1490–1500, oil on panel, National Gallery, London, UK/The Bridgeman Art Library. 73.5 x 59.1 cms | 63

Figure 15–19: *Five Angels for the Millennium,* 2001

Video/sound installation

Five channels of color video projection on walls in large, dark room; stereo sound for each projection

Projected image size: 240 x 320 cm each; room dimensions variable

Performers: Josh Coxx (Panels i-iv), Andrew Tritz (Panel v)

Edition of three, with two artists proofs

Figure 15: *Five Angels for the Millennium,* 2001 | 65

Video/sound installation

i. "Departing Angel"

Performer: Josh Coxx

Figure 16: *Five Angels for the Millennium,* 2001 | 65

Video/sound installation

ii. "Birth Angel"

Performer: Josh Coxx

Figure 17: *Five Angels for the Millennium*, 2001 | 66
Video/sound installation
iii. "Fire Angel"
Performer: Josh Coxx

Figure 18: *Five Angels for the Millennium*, 2001 | 66
Video/sound installation
iv. "Ascending Angel"
Performer: Josh Coxx

Figure 19: *Five Angels for the Millennium*, 2001 | 67
Video/sound installation
v. "Creation Angel"
Performer: Andrew Tritz

Figure 20: *The Messenger*, 1996 | 70
Video/sound installation
Color video projection on large vertical screen mounted on wall in darkened space; amplified stereo sound
Performer: Chad Walker
Photo: Edward Woodman

Figure 21–22: *Observance*, 2002 | 75
Color High-Definition video on plasma display mounted on wall
47 ½ x 28 ½ 4 in (120.7 x 72.4 x 10.2 cm)
Performers: Alan Abelew, Sheryl Arenson, Frank Bruynbroek, Carol Cetrone, Cathy Chang, Ernie Charles, Alan Clark, JD Cullum, Michael Irby, Tanya Little, Susan Matus, Kate Noonan, Paul O'Connor, Valerie Spencer, Louis Stark, Richard Stobie, Michael Eric Strickland, Ellis Williams
10:14 minutes
Edition of five with two artist's proofs

Acknowledgments

THIS PROJECT IS THE result of countless iterations and reconsiderations over the years, and many individuals have been tremendously helpful and generous with their time, guidance and editorial acumen along the way. Its first outing was as a graduate thesis in the Department of Theology and Religious Studies at the University of Scranton, in Scranton, PA, under the able direction of Dr. Maria Poggi Johnson. Her support, encouragement and insight shepherded the project from a vague spark of an idea to its first stage of completion. Also influential along that route were Drs. Charles R. Pinches and Will T. Cohen, also at the University of Scranton. From there various chapters and portions of chapters were presented, in various stages of (in)completion, at several professional academic meetings in recent years, including the Association of Art Historians annual conference in Manchester, UK in 2009, the Association of Scholars of Christianity in the History of Art in Paris in 2010, the Museum of Biblical Art in New York in 2011, and the American Academy of Religion in San Francisco in 2011. At each step, thoughtful questions were raised and astute suggestions offered that helped to make the argument more cogent and focused. Support for travel to many of these professional venues was made possible by the generosity of the Provost's and the President's Offices of Wentworth Institute of Technology in Boston, MA, where as faculty I've also received supportive and perceptive feedback from students and colleagues.

For the editorial and production assistance in the final sprint to publication I wish to thank Christian Amondson and the wonderful—and patient—staff of Wipf and Stock Publishers.

And finally, I owe a tremendous debt of gratitude for the kindness and warm spirit of Bill Viola, Kira Perov, and their assistant, Christen

Sperry-Garcia of Bill Viola Studio LLC, who gave generously of their time and insight as this project reached its final (for now) form.

1

Introduction

Towards a Visual Theology

For in hope we were saved. Now hope that is seen is not hope. For who hopes for what is seen? But if we hope for what we do not see, we wait for it with patience.

—ROMANS 8:24–25

THE ESTRANGEMENT OF ART from religion is one of the many unhappy legacies of Modernism. There was a time, however, when the aesthetic and the theological were of a piece. This study of selected works by American video artist Bill Viola[1] considers the possible re-emergence of a theological dimension to contemporary art, a *re-enchantment* of art some have called it, which means "stepping beyond the modern traditions of mechanism, positivism, empiricism, rationalism, materialism, secularism, and scientism—the whole objectifying consciousness of the Enlightenment and the materialistic disbelief in interiority—in a way that allows for a return of the soul."[2]

1. This study makes no claims to a comprehensive or exhaustive interpretation of the whole of Viola's output; rather, my interest is in a select group of works, seen through the lens of Christian mystical theology and the philosophical sublime, in a way that may well provide a methodological framework for investigating other examples within the artist's oeuvre, both past and ongoing.

2. Gablik, *Reenchantment of Art*, 11.

1

Long estranged from symbol and sacrament, artists seem to have turned once again to a vision rooted in the soul, where "soul" may be understood, in a Hegelian sense, as that which transcends individuality and bonds us with other people and communities—art as a way of *re-humanizing* us, summoning us to a rekindled humanity and a social instinct of empathy with others, what Viola himself has described as an "awareness" that may counter the "anti-human" tendencies in today's world.[3] Something on this order may be what philosopher Henri Bergson had in mind in his lesser-known treatise of 1932, *The Two Sources of Morality and Religion*, in which he characterized human life has having two tendencies, "closed" and "open." While the former tends toward boundedness, exclusivity, self-preservation, individuality, group solidarity, and stability, the latter inclines to openness, love, inclusion, and care that reach beyond the limited bounds of the individual or group.[4] Soul, or spirit, understood in this context, is ultimately social, one's sense of participation and membership in a shared humanity or community, a social instinct of sympathy with the Other—a "yearning" the artist calls it.[5] Viola has himself remarked, "One of the greatest dangers in our lives today is the objective eye . . . Rational objectivity is distancing us from the moral, emotional responsibility that we have towards other human beings. The detached eye is a dangerous instrument."[6] In an era marked culturally by world-weary cynicism and solipsistic and self-conscious irony, a new paradigm may be emerging within an artistic practice that has grown increasingly uncomfortable with its inherited condition of "unbelief" and has re-committed itself to a project of restoring theology to aesthetics.

Quite to the contrary, however, contemporary theorist Thierry de Duve has argued for a continued faith in the Enlightenment project that others have generally agreed has failed us; de Duve's hope is that artists *not* engage lingering interests in spirituality, maintaining that "the best modern art has endeavored to redefine the essentially *religious* terms of humanism on *belief-less* bases."[7] "Belief," as it is invoked here, is understood as the modern notion of intellectual assent, with onto-theological implications; that is different, I shall contend, from an understanding of belief as faith and faith as trust, as the substance of things hoped for, as we are reminded by Paul in his letter to the Romans in the epigraph to this chapter. Postmodern religion scholar Marc C. Taylor, goes further, and identifies what he calls a

---

3. Author's interview with Bill Viola and Kira Perov on August 19, 2013.

4. Lefebvre and White, *Bergson, Politics, and Religion*.

5. Interview, August 19, 2013.

6. Raney, "Interview with Bill Viola," in Raney, *Art in Question*, 84.

7. Duve, *Look: 100 Years of Contemporary Art*, 14.

theoesthetic "in which art and religion join to lead individuals and society from fragmentation and opposition to integration and unification."[8] Clearly the matter is not resolved. "Art and faith," arbitrates William Dyrness, "both strain at the boundaries in which they are placed. They slip out of our grasp because they both deal in wonder. Maybe our conversation," he continues, "ought at least to remember this fact, and acknowledge that both are, ultimately, not within our control. That would be a start. All sides, it would seem, have much to gain from such humility."[9]

In the introduction to his popular 2004 study, *On the Strange Place of Religion in Contemporary Art*, art historian and theorist James Elkins succinctly describes my own sense of professional unease in pursuing this topic: "For people in my profession of art history," Elkins confesses, "the very fact that I have written this book may be enough to cast me into a dubious category of fallen and marginal historians who somehow don't get modernism or postmodernism."[10] The art world, he claims, "can accept a wide range of 'religious' art by people who hate religion, by people who are deeply uncertain about it, by the disgruntled and the disaffected and the skeptical, but there is no place for artists who express straightforward, ordinary religious faith."[11] There is, the critic is saying, a general tendency within the art world to see art that invokes religion in any but a critical or sardonic way as retrograde and reactionary. "[T]he absence of openly religious art from modern art museums," Elkins further contends, "would seem to be due to the prejudices of a coterie of academic writers who have become unable to acknowledge what has always been apparent: art and religion are entwined."[12] Yet, as John Walsh, Director Emeritus of the J. Paul Getty Museum in Los Angeles, has argued, Bill Viola "stands outside the tight embrace of critical theory and art production. His art has little or no irony, does not refer to other contemporary art, and is unabashedly devoted to the 'great themes.'"[13] Viola is, I would add, one of the few artists today willing to reaffirm the spiritual in a world in which it is increasingly difficult to gain a critical distance from the tyranny of the material and to think of transcendence at all.[14]

8. Taylor, *Disfiguring*, 46.

9. Elkins and Morgan, *Re-Enchantment*, 229.

10. Elkins, *On the Strange Place of Religion in Contemporary Art*, xi.

11. Ibid.

12. Ibid.

13. Walsh, *Bill Viola*, 57.

14. It must be said upfront that, in my recent interview with Viola, the artist made clear that his interests were less in religion and theology, or in any one particular religion, and more in the spiritual and its cultural manifestations.

The present contribution to the discussion aims to challenge that assumed secularism of institutional art history—what Sally M. Promey describes as the "secularlization theory of modernity" which contends that "modernism necessarily leads to religion's decline, and the secular and the religious will not coexist in the modern world,"[15] and what Hans Belting labels the "paradigm of art history."[16] My study aims to resist the pervasive skepticism when it comes to religion as a topic of discussion in the academy, to move beyond our contemporary and unhelpful model of the secular left (militant atheism) and evangelical right (dogmatic theism), and to come to terms with faith as an irrecusable part of the fabric of the social. More specifically, my purpose is to speculate on the place of the sacred in contemporary visual culture, and, in doing so, to consider the key features of any contemporary theological aesthetics—that it be revelatory and transformative. Bill Viola's art, I shall argue, provokes the possibility of just such theological reflection.

Fortunately, a much welcome new publication, *ReVisioning: Critical Methods of Seeing Christianity in the History of Art*, edited by historians James Romaine and Linda Stratford, brings together more than a dozen essays by both emerging and established scholars, which collectively seek to expand the discourse on Christianity in the history of art, in part by challenging the equation of modernism with secularism as a methodological approach to the writing of art history. Romaine writes in the book's Introduction:

> The prevailing narrative of art history is one that charts a movement from the sacred to the secular, progressing out of past historical periods in which works of art were produced to reveal, embrace, and glorify the divine and toward a modern conception of art as materialist and a more recent emphasis on social context. In fact, for many art historians this secularization of art is not only a narrative within the history of art; it has been the narrative of art history as an academic field. Some interpretations of twentieth and twentieth-first century art not only insist on equating modernism with secularism but also describe the erasure of all mention of spiritual presence from the scholarly discourse as a triumph for the field of art history.[17]

The present study seeks to contest that narrative and to contribute to an emerging field that still lacks the methodological framework by which to honestly and meaningfully address art's engagement with theology, or at

15. Promey, "'Return' of Religion," 48.

16. Belting, *Art History after Modernism*, vii.

17. Romaine and Stratford, *ReVisioning*, 5.

the very least with a religious awareness that, as Dyrness put it, "slips away in the very effort to grasp it." The theological framework I will engage here begins with the ancient tradition of *apophatic*, or negative, theology—God talk" ("theo"—"logy") that seeks to describe God only in terms of what may not be said about God, what God is *not*. This is the topic of my second chapter. In the words of 9th-century mystic John the Scot Eriugena: "We do not know what God is. God Himself does not know what He is because He is not anything. Literally God is not, because He transcends being."[18]

Chapter three will then go on to theorize this transcendence within the context of the Sublime,[19] that which critic and philosopher Arthur Danto claims "rocked . . . [the] self-congratulatory culture of the Enlightenment."[20] It is in the presence of the sublime where we witness the straining of the mind at the edges of itself and at the borders of discursive reasoning, prompting a mode of reverence for the inexpressible, the unspeakable. And it is the technology of video, a medium freed from the usual spatio-temporal constraints of plastic art, that enables Bill Viola, David Jasper argues, to "negotiate these sacramental moments in crossings of space and time, breathless moments of eternity in which our being is both slowed and quickened . . ."[21] In the sublime's reemergence in the postmodern world, I shall argue, this very experience of disproportion between the mind's conceptualizing power and an ungraspable complexity, serves as an analogue for or intuition of something else—the infinite, the divine—and thus the promises of transcendence.

From this acknowledgment of desire or hope or yearning, French postmodern thinkers—Emmanuel Levinas, Jean-François Lyotard, Jacques Derrida, and Jean-Luc Marion, among others—will have something to offer my argument, having themselves taken a "theological turn." As such, Viola's art will be considered here as a theological enterprise, located in a tradition that runs from the medieval and Early Christian apophatics to postmodern deconstructors. Using the high-tech apparatus of modern video—high speed film, high definition video, LCD and plasma screens, and sophisticated sound recording—American artist Bill Viola's work has roots in the theological tradition of transcendent experience. All are put to use by the artist in ways that significantly challenge prevailing artistic traditions and

18. John the Scot Eriugena, in Franke, *On What Cannot Be Said*, 1:186.

19. As this study relies heavily on the work of James Elkins, it is incumbent on me to acknowledge at the outset Elkins's most recent rejection of the sublime in such a context as an inefficient and moribund category, as "weak" and "damaged goods." It will be obvious to the reader that I do not follow him here. See Elkins, "Against the Sublime," in Hoffman and Whyte, *Beyond the Finite*, 75–90.

20. Danto, *Abuse of Beauty*, 148.

21. Townsend, *Art of Bill Viola*, 118.

return art to the power of the sublime, to an aesthetic of revelation, and to an inquiry into transcendence. In dealing with the idea of representing the invisible, Viola's art converges, I suggest, with postmodern notions of the "unrepresentable." Chapter four will consider a number of specific examples of Viola's work in order to test the theological adequacy of the sublime as heuristic, chiefly within the context of contemporary postmodern culture, and to lay the groundwork for a theory and practice of an *ethical sublime*.

While the aesthetic sublime was introduced into 20th-century mainstream art theory and practice decades ago by the environmentally-scaled canvases of Abstract Expressionist painters and spiritual provocateurs such as Barnett Newman (author of "The Sublime is Now," 1948) and Mark Rothko, modern video, as a time-based medium is especially suited to this aesthetic category. Yet Rothko may be instructive here, particularly in his theorizing about his floating fields of color, where nearly imperceptible shifts of tone, intensity and saturation are observable only in prolonged looking—as "gates" or doors through which the beholder might imaginatively leave the world of matter, and enter a realm of ultimacy: "I am interested only in expressing the basic human emotions," he said, "tragedy, ecstasy, doom, and so on . . . The people who weep before my pictures are having the same religious experience I had when I painted them."[22] The impassioned language of "tragedy," "ecstasy," "agony," and "bliss" is not unlike, as we will see, the emotionally descriptive language of Viola. James Elkins in his fascinating study, *Pictures and Tears: A History of People Who Have Cried in Front of Paintings*, confirms of Rothko: ". . . you may find yourself *inside* [the canvas]." "It is not hard to see why people say they are overwhelmed," he continues:

> Everything conspires to overload the senses: the empty incandescent rectangles of color, entirely encompassing your field of vision; the sheer glowing silence; the lack of footing, or anything solid, in the world of the canvas; the weird sense that the color is very far away, yet suffocatingly close. It's not a pleasant feeling: you feel both threatened and comforted . . .[23]

We should take note here of the phenomenology of suffering and threat, challenges to one's sense of security, safety, and earthbound sanctuary. The sublime is both inviting and fearsome.

Disembodied color for Rothko, in its boundlessness and separation from (withholding of) the represented object—that is, the negation of figuration, contour, narrative and even of space—and the stripping away of

22 López-Remiro, *Writings on Art*, 133ff.

23. Elkins, *Pictures and Tears*, 18.

incident in Barnett Newman's monochrome fields, seem to transcend the material environment in which they appear, establishing an amorphousness that is immeasurable and unquantifiable, with the numinous potency of nothingness, which for these artists was profoundly spiritual. This is echoed in both the words and images, particularly in the Black Paintings, of Rothko's and Newman's contemporary Ad Reinhardt, and in his poetic positionings against the "idolatry" of all external representation.

> Leave temple images behind
> Risen above beauty, beyond virtues, inscrutable, indescribable
> Self-transcendence   revealed yet unrevealed
>
> Undifferentiated unity, oneness, no divisions, no multiplicity
> No consciousness of anything
> No consciousness of consciousness
>
> All distinctions disappear in darkness
> The darkness is the brilliance   numinous, resonance . . .[24]

Yet, we may reasonably ask, can such an experience be had from video, a most material, technological, and scientifically-grounded medium, yet one which, since the late 1980s has assumed a position of legitimacy, even prominence in the art world?

Bill Viola had been drawn to the nexus of art and technology as a student in the 1970s at Syracuse University, mainly as a means for exploration of the self and spiritual development. In an interview given in 1997, he remembers:

> Something that has been a part of me as long as I can remember [is] the excitement of the new technique. I grew up in a postwar generation. A big influence on me was the World's Fair in New York in 1964–65, which was about as close to industrial Utopia as you can get. For me it was essentially a bunch of dark rooms with images projected in them, a series of installations, but cast in "technology is good, the future is positive" kind of mode.[25]

For artists and audiences raised in an era of media saturation, video is a way of participating in and reacting to what Jean Baudrillard, French philosopher, sociologist, and cultural theorist, referred to as the "ecstasy of communication" or the "obscenity of the visible" and its destructive work of cognitive fragmentation—he calls it a "new form of schizophrenia." The

---

24 Reinhardt in Franke, *On What Cannot Be Said*, 2:47.
25. Ross, *Bill Viola*, 152.

centrality of the television screen, for Baudrillard, forces the "promiscuity of networks" and the "total instantaneity of things" and, through overexposure, urges the "end of interiority and intimacy," where we are no more than "a switching center for all the networks of influence."[26] This is the post-Enlightenment evolution of visual modes within culture as *spectacle*. More recently, Pulitzer Prize-winning journalist and critic Chris Hedges has examined this cultural *mediocracy* in his jeremiad, *Empire of Illusion: The End of Literacy and the Triumph of Spectacle*.[27]

> The flight into illusion sweeps away the core values of the open society. It corrodes the ability to think for oneself, to draw independent conclusions, to express dissent when judgment and common sense tell you something is wrong, to be self-critical, and to acknowledge that there are other views, different ways, and structures of being that are morally and socially acceptable.[28]

Yet Viola's work, I want to suggest, uses the technology of spectacle *against* itself, in resistance and opposition to the medium's materialist attitude and this-worldly motivations. While thoroughly in accord with cultural critics like Hedges on the intellectual and spiritual degradations of contemporary media saturation, Viola urges:

> The big responsibility right now is to develop an understanding and awareness of the effects these images have. We are in a situation now culturally, whereby the people who have created this huge machine which is inundating us, flooding us with images—every night every hour every day all around us—have no knowledge or awareness or understanding of the real effect those images are going to have on us . . . The entire society is illiterate, and they are being controlled by the people who can read, that is the controllers of these images, the image-makers.[29]

As a time-based medium, video art allows for manipulations of the ordinary experience of time; it is a non-narrative time which in Viola's work is represented in the form of large, slow-moving, mesmerizing images; it is an art of duration and absorption, through which the artist shows us "the hidden dimension of our lives" and a return to interiority. "Human beings," the artist argues, "as all living beings, are essentially creations of

26. Jean Baudrillard, "The Ecstasy of Communication," in Foster, *Postmodern Culture*, 128.

27. Hedges, *Empire of Illusion*.

28. Ibid., 52.

29. Viola, in Campbell, "Bill Viola," 91.

time.”[30] Exploiting the possibilities of electronic technology, Viola, we will see, creates a disrupted representation and de-familiarized embodiment of movement and time—slow motion, time-lapse, acceleration and deceleration—to explore the dimensions of the human condition and to encounter the "unseen." Indeed it may be argued that video (and perhaps even the Internet) has provided a technological base for religion's re-entry into public awareness.

We are, then, returned to the question with which we began, prompted as it was by James Elkins's modest but fertile examination of "the strange place of religion in contemporary art:" Is it possible thinking past the mutual mistrust of art and religion, to re-read and re-engage spiritual themes within postmodern culture? Is it possible to propose an alternative perspective on the "human condition," one that speculates on the place of the numinous and a life of faith in contemporary art and culture, and opens up the field of inquiry to include appreciation of affective nuances of lived encounter? In effect, the goal of this study will be to test the adequacy of visual culture to lived human experience and to the deeply felt life, and in so doing to consider the key features of any contemporary theological aesthetics—that it be revelatory, participatory, and transformative. We return to Elkins's eloquent reminder that we must continue to reflect on the relation between visual culture and the sacred: "It is impossible to talk sensibly about religion and at the same time address art in an informed and intelligent manner: but it is also irresponsible not to keep trying."[31]

In that which is hidden, I shall argue, Viola offers moments for a self-revealing divine. He will be read, then, as a theologian whose medium is light, movement and sound, rather than words; and while my focus here is on the Christian strain of that visual theology, it is important to note—and I will do so where appropriate—that the artist's deep familiarity with and expressions of the divine across a number of faith traditions, both Western and Eastern, inform his work. I will approach the work as offering a phenomenology of hope, such that we, as beholders, remain receptively open to the overwhelming possibility, indeed the promise, of the "appearance" of God. Further, this study will develop a method for what James Romaine calls a "critical-devotional reading" of visual theology which "takes seriously the nature of religious art as sacramental, revelatory, and inspirational."[32]

---

30. Viola, *Reasons for Knocking*, 278.

31. Elkins, *On the Strange Place of Religion*, 116. See also Heartney, *Postmodern Heretics.*

32. Romaine and Stratford, *ReVisioning*, 17.

While the argument will largely address Viola's more recent and allusive installations, it is necessary to my story to begin with an earlier, and I believe most seminal piece, more narrative by comparison to the later works, which will introduce my narrative's main threads. It is an installation I first encountered in the 1996 exhibition at the Museum of Contemporary Art in Chicago, *Negotiating Rapture: The Power of Art to Transform Lives*, a major exhibition that took the rather unusual position (at the time) of seeking to revive the sacerdotal role of the artist in the postmodern era. In this exhibition, Viola joined the ranks of such luminaries as Joseph Beuys, Francis Bacon, Anselm Kiefer, Barnett Newman, and Ad Reinhardt, among others. Viola's contribution to that exhibition was his 1983 installation *Room for St. John of the Cross*, the work to which we now turn.

2

In the Dark Night of the Soul

Room for St. John of the Cross

I entered I knew not where and abided without knowing,
transcending all knowledge.

—ST. JOHN OF THE CROSS, "THE DARK NIGHT"

IN 1983, BILL VIOLA first exhibited the sound and video installation, *Room for St. John of the Cross* (see Figure 1), a spatial, temporal and aural environment comprised of a small black box enclosure—approximately 6 x 5 x 5.5 feet—confined within a larger darkened room, itself measuring 14 x 24 x 30 feet; on one side of the enclosure is a small window through which glows a soft incandescent light. As viewers approach, stoop and peer through the small aperture, rather awkwardly, like a penitent in a confessional, into an otherwise inaccessible room of white walls and dirt floor—a room minimally furnished with a wooden table on which are arranged a pitcher, a glass of water, and a four-inch color video monitor—they hear the barely audible incantation, in Spanish, of St. John's love poetry.

Figure 1.

Figure 2.

Composed between 1577 and 1578, the religious reformer created this work while imprisoned for nine months in a space the same size as the cubicle and subjected, through daily torture, to what he called his "dark night of the soul." That "night" was a profound dread-filled experience of abandonment, not only by his faith community but by God himself, as if God had turned away and "left him to dissolve painfully into the dark void of his prison cell."[1] It was from this intense feeling of abjection and solitude, however, that St. John composed this most passionate poetry, in which he speaks of an inpouring of grace, of profound and ecstatic love experienced as an imagined journey through the night, soaring over city walls and mountain peaks. Outside the small cell, in Viola's re-staging, viewers are unsteadied by a quaking large-screen video projection of a snow-covered mountain range filmed in black and white, exteriorizing the sensation of boundless and weightless flight, and all this accompanied by the unrelenting roar of wind and white noise saturating the room. Meanwhile, on the small video monitor inside the cell (see Figure 2), another mountain view glows quietly and motionless in vivid color as natural light shifts in real space and time. At once viewers are made to feel their own incarceration in the larger room, invited to imagine the imprisoned reformer, and to contemplate the meaning of his (and our) suffering in worldly confinement. For St. John of the Cross—as for us—from this isolation and privation will come inwardness and introspection, from negation of the self in *this* world will come contact with transcendence and with an all-consuming love latent in the self that endures suffering. Indeed, Viola remembers that, as a young artist in 1983, this piece marked a turning point in his life, a "coming out" he's called it, creating a work amidst "intense" criticism, based on the suffering and ordeal of a Christian saint ("everything those guys hate"), and a declaration of sorts, despite the prevailing winds of criticism, that as an artist he had an interest in spiritual things.[2]

The Apophatic Tradition in Christian Mysticism

In a 1997 interview, Viola remarked on his discovery of the figures of Early Christianity and the 16th-century mystics John of the Cross and his mentor Teresa of Avila, as well as the earlier 14th-century Dominican German monk Meister Eckhart and the anonymous author of the medieval text, *The Cloud of Unknowing*, all within the Christian tradition of the *via negativa*:

1. Morgan in Townsend, *Art of Bill Viola*, 104. I lean here on Morgan's vivid description.
2. Interview August 19, 2013.

The *via negativa* in the West is connected to a shadowy fifth-century character known as Pseudo-Dionysius the Aeropagite, who . . . described an immanent God . . . as opposed to the transcendent God of the more familiar *via positiva*, over and above all and outside the individual. The *via positiva* describes God as the ultimate expression of a series of attributes or qualities—good, all-seeing, all-knowing, etc.—of which human beings contain lesser, diminished versions . . . The *via negativa*, on the other hand, is the way of negation. God is wholly other and cannot be described or comprehended. There are no attributes other than unknowability. When the mind faces the divine reality, it seizes up and enters a "cloud of unknowing," or to use St. John of the Cross' term, "a dark night of the soul." Here in the darkness, the only thing to go on is faith, and the only way to approach God is from within, primarily through love. This is why much of St. John's poetry reads like classic love poems.[3]

Here Viola threads a connection, as he understands it, between the 16th-century saints John of the Cross and Teresa of Avila and their medieval mystic forebears, tracing the history back even further to Pseudo-Dionysius the Areopagite in the ancient fabric of *apophatic theology*—that is, a speaking of God only in terms of what may *not* be said about God, a "negative theology," often allied with, but not reducible to, the intuitive approaches of mysticism.

Negative theology, as Ilse Bulhof and Laurens ten Kate amongst others have shown, is an ancient tradition the sources for which are found in late antiquity reaching as far back as Plato's *Parmenides* and the early Christian era with Gregory of Nyssa (4th century), St. Augustine (4th-5th century), attaining its first significant high point in the Neoplatonic philosophy of the 3rd century CE, with yet more radical representations found among the mystics of the early-to-late Middle Ages, from Johanes Scotus Eriugena (9th century) to Thomas Aquinas (13th century).[4] Aphophatic theology is a form of discourse that fundamentally consists of language that negates itself in order to evoke that which is beyond words, beyond the limits of saying altogether. "'Apophasis' reads etymologically," explains William Franke, "as 'away from speech' or 'saying away' (*apo*, 'from' or 'away from'; *phasis*, 'assertion,' from *phemi*, 'assert' or 'say'), and this points in the direction of unsaying and ultimately of silence."[5] Apophasis is, paradoxically, a

3. Ross, *Bill Viola*, 144.

4. Bulhof and ten Kate, *Flight of the Gods*, 4–5. See also William Franke's two-volume edited study, *On What Cannot Be Said: Apophatic Discourses in Philosophy, Religion, Literature, and the Arts.*

5. Franke, *On What Cannot Be Said*, 2.

rich genre of theological discourse that articulates the utter inefficacy of the Logos to name ultimate reality. This tradition is fostered by a notion fundamentally opposed to the central tenet of classical Greek philosophy of Being (or ontology) and its claims for autonomous human reason; rather, says apophatics, what human desire truly seeks—the divine—cannot be defined, pronounced, or known because it is radically transcendent, incommensurably *Other*, beyond the (human) subject and outside the limits of rationality and the hubris of classical metaphysics.

Negative theology's emphasis on the unknowableness and the unutterableness of the Divine informs the notion that "transcendence is best approached via denials, via what according to earthly concepts *is not*. Hence the name 'negative theology.'"[6] Denying what is given and speaking in contradictions is the very means for communicating transcendent or hidden realities. "The apophatic," argues theologian Denys Turner, "is the linguistic strategy of somehow showing by means of language that which lies beyond language."[7] Thus, for St. John of the Cross, silence and the experience of divine *absence* is understood to be the veiled *presence* of divine fullness— for in hiddenness is revelation.[8] "[R]evelation is nothing more than the disclosure of some hidden truth," writes St. John.[9] Put another way, rather than a *concept* of God, negative theology looks to a positive and intimate *experience* of God and theological insight into the ineffability of God. While ineffable, God *is* encountered.

In language, Turner further argues, this deliberate refusal of a materialist clarity is precisely what appeals in medieval mysticism to postmodern thought and to a contemporary apophatic revival, with its "messages of the decentering and fragmentation of knowledge, of the collapse of stable relations between cognitive subjects and the objects of their knowledge, of the destablizations of fixed relations between signifier and signified."[10]

Regarding the inadequacy of linguistic communication itself, regardless of its intended reference (sacred or secular), founding father of deconstruction Jacques Derrida has famously argued the case against "an intimate link between sound and sense," against the "inward and immediate realization of meaning which yields itself up without reserve to perfect, transcendent understanding;" in its place he posits the recognition of an infinity of meanings deferred, an "endless displacement of meaning which governs

---

6. Bulhof and ten Kate, *Flight of the Gods*, 5.

7. Turner, *Darkness of God*, 34.

8. See also in this context Davies and Turner, *Silence and the Word*.

9. Kavanaugh and Rodrigues, *Collected Works of Saint John of the Cross*, 244.

10. Turner, "Art of Unknowing," 473.

language and places it forever beyond the reach of stable, self-authenticating knowledge."[11] We will have occasion later to assess this view of the (in) adequacy of language seemingly shared between apophatic theology and postmodernist deconstruction and, more specifically, to mark the crucial distinctions between them—and where Viola aligns himself. While there are indeed certain resonances between these epistemologies, the distinctions between them will require clarification. But first, it is important to draw a closer connection between John of the Cross, his own Reformation context, and the traces of such in Viola's 1983 installation.

St. John of the Cross and Mystic Forebears

As a founder, along with Teresa of Avila, of the reformist order the Discalced ("Barefoot") Carmelites, John of the Cross (Juan de Yepes, 1542–1591) was imprisoned in Toledo by his superiors in December of 1577 for his refusal to desist in reform efforts within the Carmelite order, particularly amidst the fervor of the Catholic Counter-Reformation.[12] Incarcerated for nine months, he was subjected to regular torture and public flogging, managing to escape in August of 1578. During that time, seeking relief he composed the greater part of his poem *Spiritual Canticle*, a symbolic variation on the *Song of Songs* (itself filled with lyrical images of mountains, valleys and rivers, not unfamiliar to the symbology of the sublime). The *Canticle* narrates the nighttime journey of a bride (the human soul) as she searches for her lost lover (Christ): "Faith and love will lead you along a path unknown to you, to the place where God is hidden," the Saint writes. The story unfolds as a dialogue between the two lovers and tells of a love that moves forward in degrees or stages and through experiences of restlessness, incompleteness, impediment and various other "wounds of love," to ultimate consummation in spiritual union. The Bride's "dark night of the soul" narrates the hardships and difficulties she endures in her progressive detachment from the world—a detachment characterized as the deprivation of sensible appetites for external things of the material world and gratifications of the will—all toward reaching the light of union with her lover; it is a painful experience of spiritual maturation, through loss, dissolution and the transformation of the self toward ultimate union with God. And just as in darkness there is privation of light, this journey demands—common also to Jewish, Islamic and Eastern strains of mysticism—privation and purgative suffering in the pursuit of unity, oneness, or identity with spiritual truth or God.

11. Norris, *Deconstruction*, 28–29.

12. Kavanaugh and Rodrigues, *Collected Works*, passim.

A Poetic and Mystical Tradition

It is not incidental that arguably St. John's greatest work he titled *The Ascent of Mount Carmel*—"ascent" of the soul from the crudities of this limited world and the attachment to things, ideas, and one's own self; and "Mount Carmel," the place where Elijah called down the true God to overthrow the claims of idolaters (1 Kgs 18:20–40). Verses 11 and 12 read: "Now there was a great wind, so strong that it was splitting mountains and breaking rocks in pieces before the Lord, but the Lord was not in the wind; and after the wind an earthquake, but the Lord was not in the earthquake; and after the earthquake a fire, but the Lord was not in the fire; and after the fire a sound of sheer silence."

St. John's work begins as a mystical poem that treats of sensual purgation and gives an account of the soul's ascetical search for, and movement toward, perfect union; here the poet chronicles the ineffable mystical experiences along the way toward encounter with the Divine experienced in contemplation, and described as withdrawal from the world and, ultimately, ecstatic union:

> *In a dark night,*
> *My longing heart, aglow with love,*
> *– Oh, blessed lot! –*
> *I went forth unseen*
> *From my house that was at last in deepest rest.*
>
> *Secure and protected by darkness,*
> *I climbed the secret ladder, in disguise,*
> *– Oh, blessed lot! –*
> *In darkness, veiled and concealed I went*
> *Leaving behind my house in deepest rest.*
>
> *Oh, blissful night!*
> *Oh, secret night, when I remained unseeing and unseen,*
> *When the flame burning in my heart*
> *Was my only light and guide.*
>
> *This inward light,*
> *A safer guide than nooonday's brightness,*
> *Showed me the place where He awaited me*
> *– My soul's Beloved –*

A place of solitude.

Oh, night that guided me!
Oh, night more lovely than the rosy dawn!
Oh, night whose darkness guided me
To that sweet union,
In which the lover and Beloved are made one.

Upon the flower of my breast,
Kept undefiled for Him alone,
He fell asleep,
While I was waking
Caressing Him with gentle cedars' breeze.

And when Aurora's breath
Began to spread His curled hair,
His gentle hand
He placed upon my neck.
And all my senses were in bliss suspended.

Forgetful of myself,
My head reclined on my Beloved,
The world was gone
And all my cares at rest,
Forgotten all my grief among the lilies.[13]

It is significant to the present study that St. John sought to express mystical experience by means of poetry, suggestive of the prosaic indescribability of the experience. Unlike prose, poetic language is not limited by a sense of mimetic adequacy to external "reality;" rather, it dispenses with precise description and employs allusion and suggestion. Whereas prose legislates syntactical order and hierarchizes its linguistic components to effect precision and clarity, poetry gears discourse not toward logical sequence and narrative order but rather toward disjunction and connotative obscurity, its subject less immediately and concretely available to perception and only more gradually and evocatively suggested through its presentation in the description. The argument here is that poetic language may reveal the nature of things with an intensity and comprehensiveness lacking in ordinary language, a content not immediately available to linguistic/auditory perception.

13. Reinhardt, *St. John of the Cross*, 1–3.

The business of poetry, in other words, is to take one beyond the mere description and presentation of objects in the world; it has the distinctive feature of being absolutely self-conscious about language as its medium, employing that language in such a way that turns the hearer's attention back onto it, not merely describing but evaluating the subject it addresses by forcing the hearer to engage with that subject through heightened concentration on the self-imposing language in description, and even to enjoy its artistry. It is a thickening of the verbal medium which involves the manipulation of words, phrases, and syntax wherein enumeration, sequence, and the uniform patterns of description—the "rational" form of language—are eliminated in favor of unfamiliar inversions of words, neologisms, broken phrases, ellipses, and deviations from and disruptions of the connectiveness of syntax. It is a matter of refusing traditional usage, forcing obscurity and disrupting immediate access to the subject—*slowing* access to that subject— yet generating fresh senses beyond the range of ordinary uses of language and thereby forcing our uncommon attentiveness to the language in description, and an uncommon sensitivity to the subject *because of* the very disruption of our habitual attention to it, *because of* the language in which it is formulated. As contemporary literary theorist David Scott has put it, "a radical change in the structure or ordering of syntax implies a corresponding shift in perspective in viewing the world. This is because the relationship between the order of syntax in language and the order of perception of phenomena in reality, as expressed in description, are closely bound up."[14] And as such it is, at least as deployed by John of the Cross, apophatic. St. John explains his approach to language in the Prologue to *The Spiritual Canticle*:

> . . . the Holy Spirit, unable to express the fullness of His meaning in ordinary words, utters mysteries in strange figures and likenesses . . . [T]he abundant meanings of the Holy Spirit cannot be caught in words . . . Since these stanzas, then, were composed in a love flowing from abundant mystical understanding, I cannot explain them adequately, nor is it my intention to do so . . . This communication is secret and dark to the work of the intellect . . . Since this interior wisdom is so simple, general, and spiritual that in entering the intellect it is not clothed in any sensory species or image, the imaginative faculty cannot form an idea or picture of it in order to speak of it . . . The language of God has this trait: Since it is very spiritual and intimate to the soul, transcending everything sensory, it immediately silences the entire ability and harmonious composite of the exterior and interior senses . . . Since the wisdom of this contemplation is the

14. Scott, *Pictorialist Poetics*, 32.

language of God to the soul, the Pure Spirit to the spirit alone, all that is less than spirit such as the sensory, fails to perceive it. Consequently this wisdom is secret to the senses; they have neither the knowledge nor ability to speak of it, nor do they even desire to do so because it is beyond words.[15]

Similar in tone and structure to *The Ascent of Mount Carmel* is St. John's *The Living Flame of Love*, an ecstatic expression of what is ultimately indefinable—the pursuit of a transcendent, unitive and noetic experience with absolute reality:

> *I entered into unknowing,*
> *and there I remained unknowing*
> transcending all knowledge.
>
> *I entered into unknowing,*
> *yet when I saw myself there,*
> *without knowing where I was,*
> *I understood great things;*
> *I will not say what I felt*
> *for I remained in unknowing*
> transcending all knowledge.
> . . .
> *I was so 'whelmed,*
> *so absorbed and withdrawn,*
> *that my senses were left*
> *deprived of all their sensing,*
> *and my spirit was given*
> *an understanding while not understanding,*
> transcending all knowledge.
> . . .
> *The higher he ascends*
> *the less he understands,*
> *because the cloud is dark*
> *which lit up the night;*
> *whoever knows this*
> *remains always in unknowing*
> transcending all knowledge.

---

15. Franke, *On What Cannot Be Said*, 368–70 passim.

This knowledge in unknowing
is so overwhelming
that wise men disputing
can never overthrow it,
for their knowledge does not reach
to the understanding of not understanding,
transcending all knowledge.

And this supreme knowledge is so exalted
that no power of man or learning
can grasp it;
he who masters himself
will, with knowledge in unknowing,
always be transcending.[16]

In apophatic or negative theology, it is in these terms—"transcending all knowledge," a knowing that is, conceptually, inaccessible to "men disputing"—that the Divine is beyond words, an abstract experience that can only be recognized or intuited; human beings cannot describe the essence of God, and therefore all descriptions, if attempted, will be by necessity false. And this failure or loss of speech manifests a negation of human capacities and an annihilation of the self.[17] William Franke explains:

> Linguistic apophasis thus appears as nothing but an expression for apophasis as a condition and a dynamic of negation and self-annihilation that remains indefinable and unutterable. It cannot be formulated adequately in linguistic terms, not even as 'what cannot be said,' but can only be practiced in the wordless straining of the soul trained upon what it can neither know nor say.[18]

Again, we can turn to St. John directly: "Since God is inaccessible, be careful not to concern yourself with all that your faculties can comprehend or your senses feel, so that you do not become satisfied with less and lose the lightness of soul suitable for going to him."[19]

Neither existence *nor* nonexistence as we understand it applies to God; in this sense, God is beyond existing or, as contemporary philosopher Jean-Luc Marion will have it, "God without Being." In other words, God, the divine, or to use the terminology of the postmodern, the "Wholly Other,"

---

16. In Kavanaugh and Rodrigues, *Collected Works*, 53–54.
17. Franke, *On What Cannot Be Said*, 365.
18. Ibid.
19. Kavanaugh and Rodrigues, *Collected Works*, 89.

is not a creation, not conceptually definable in terms of space and location, and not conceptually confinable to assumptions of temporality.

Yet it is *not* nothing. Again as William Franke has argued, "this very nullity is itself something. We conceive of something which we cannot conceive . . . Our conceiving and saying relates itself to what cannot be conceived or said. The capacity for such relating (without concepts and language) can be verified as an existential fact by every individual who attempts, for example, to conceive of 'God' . . ."[20] There is still *something*, an encounter which defies talking about; but to talk about it we must still try. Such "Ultimate Reality," as Bulhof and ten Kate account for it, "is inaccessible to human thinking, inexpressible in human language, invisible to human eyes, unimaginable for the human mind"[21]—but at the same time, I would add, it is an experience there for the having, if one knows how to seek it.

Much of Bill Viola's work is precisely about that cultivation of individual experience of inexpressible divine reality as beyond the realm or limits of ordinary perception. In an interview published in 1993, the artist sounds a familiar note:

> The basic tenets of the Via Negativa are the unknowability of God: that God is wholly other, independent, complete; that God cannot be grasped by the human intellect, cannot be described in any way; that when the mind faces the divine reality, it becomes blank. It seizes up. It enters a cloud of unknowing. When the eyes cannot see, then the only thing to go on is faith, and the only true way to approach God is from within. From that point the only way God can be reached is though love. By love the soul enters into union with God, a union not infrequently described through the metaphor of ecstatic sex. Eastern religions call it enlightenment.[22]

Room for St. John of the Cross is a dramatic metaphor for solitude, anguish and abjection as sources of strength, conveyed through the dialectic of nature's terrifying tumult and the mind's inner tranquility. As historian David Morgan has put it: "Viola's installations bear the conviction that the conditions of traditional religious ritual can be simulated in works of art, in order to achieve something of the spiritual transformation wrought in the original context."[23] And in a note published in 1982, while the artist was still at work on the piece, Viola himself confirmed: "Initiation rites and age-old

20. Franke, *On What Cannot Be Said*, 17.

21. Bulhof and ten Kate, *Flight of the Gods*, 6.

22. Townsend, *Art of Bill Viola*, 131.

23. Ibid., 105.

spiritual training ordeals . . . are all controlled, staged accidents, ancient technologies designed to bring the organism to a life-threatening crisis."[24]

This life-threatening crisis and its spiritual dimension, I shall argue in the following chapter, invoke the rich philosophical tradition of the *sublime*, and more specifically its basic duality of pain and pleasure. Viola's art investigates our human condition as embodied beings, and urges us toward the experience of vulnerability, longing but ill-equipped for transcendence and ultimate renunciation of self, and it does so via the ancient traditions of mysticism and, more specifically, via *apophatic* theology and the idea that God is best identified in terms of "hiddenness" and "revelation." This, ultimately, will have resonance in contemporary notions of "negation" and "excess" as developed in continental philosophy and in particular in postmodern deconstructive critiques of Enlightenment ideals. First, however, it is important to trace its Early Christian foundations, as called upon by Viola himself.

The Dionysian Tradition

In the 1993 and 1997 interviews cited above, Viola makes frequent reference to Pseudo-Dionysius the Areopagite, the anonymous theologian and philosopher of the late 5th to early 6th century who was at one time erroneously identified as Dionysius the Areopagite, the Athenian convert of St. Paul mentioned in Acts 17:34, and in 1 Timothy 6:16, where Paul says of God: "It is he alone who has immortality and dwells in unapproachable light, whom no one has ever seen or can see." "Pseudo-Dionysius" is now widely supposed to have been a Syrian monk, who formulates one of the first articulations of apophatic theology.

In Dionysius' canonical treatise *De Divinus Nominibus* (*The Divine Names*)—a text with strong Neoplatonic influence that grew to be immensely popular amongst medieval theologians—beauty is identified as an attribute of God and inseparably conjoined with the Good. It is an idea based on Plato's notion, set out in the *Timeaus*, that the world is the product of a rational, purposive design, and that it is meant to be a good environment for human beings and non-human entities, which have themselves been deliberately produced (created) by that greater intelligence that designed the world. Plato's *Timeaus* concludes:

> For with this our world has received its full complement of living creatures, mortal and immortal, and come to be in all its

24. Ibid.

grandeur, goodness, beauty and perfection—this visible living creature made in the likeness of the intelligible and embracing all the visible, this god displayed to sense, this our heaven, one and only-begotten.[25]

This classical vision of the cosmos was then translated in the medieval world into emphatically Christian terms. Relying on Plato's distinction between physical and (unknowable) ultimate reality, Pseudo-Dionysius treated material reality as an emanation from Absolute Being, or Absolute Beauty, which transcends the whole of sensible nature but remains continuous with it in terms of "emanations" from it. The nature of the world is divine, based on eternal principles, and we—humans—can directly perceive these principles, this divinity, from reality. All created things on this view are theophanies or manifestations of God; the created world, then, presents itself to us as having order and coherence. Thus, the Good and the Beautiful are taken to be one and the same and both have their identity in God. So, in experiencing that which is beautiful in *this* world, we are experiencing the *anagogical* or "moving upward" of the mind from this world of appearances and imperfection to a contemplation of divine love. In *Mystical Theology*, Dionysius makes this even more explicit:

> The fact is that the more we take flight upward, the more our words are confined to the ideas we are capable of forming; so that now as we plunge into that darkness which is beyond intellect, we shall find ourselves not simply running short of words but actually speechless and unknowing ... [M]y argument now rises from what is below up to the transcendent, and the more it climbs, the more language falters, and when it has passed up and beyond the ascent, it will turn silent completely, since it will finally be at one with him who is indescribable.[26]

It is important here to recall Plato and the Platonic view of reality as a ladder or scale of being, and the ascent from the sensible world to the ineffable One. Recalling also Plato's Allegory of the Cave, the mystical ascent may be further characterized allegorically as a glorious ascent from darkness (illusion) to light (revelation). The Pseudo-Dionysius writes:

> ... the Superessential Beauty is called "Beauty" because of that quality which It imparts to all things severally according to their nature, and because It is the Cause of the harmony and

---

25. Plato, *Timeaus*, in Eco, *Art and Beauty*, 17.
26. Franke, *On What Cannot Be Said*, 16–17.

splendour in all things, flashing forth upon them all, like light, the beautifying communications of Its originating ray.[27]

This centrally defining metaphor of light for early Christians is thus freighted with figural implications—"seeing," "perceiving"—each with aesthetic, ethical, and spiritual dimensions. Such systematic analogy-making was a way of knowing the world; it involved both the philosophical habit of seeing the hand of God in the beauty of this world—a symbolism for the mind which perceived relations obtaining between the phenomenologies of the physical and the metaphysical—and the more conventional perception of the world as a divine work of art, such that everything in it possessed allegorical (and thus moral), in addition to literal, meanings, as if the world were designed to be interpreted for those meanings.

Yet, for Pseudo-Dionysius, divine "names" such as Beauty, Goodness, Love, Wisdom, Light, or even Being, while necessary, can be applied to God only *analogically* and therefore, in the end, inadequately; these names are both like and unlike human goodness, beauty, wisdom or being. For Dionysius—and this is the paradox of aphophatic discourse—these names are first applied to God affirmatively (that is, cataphatically)—God is of course a good, wise, beautiful and loving being—but the inadequacy of these names is also realized in their very utterance, and it is the recognition of this deficiency that leads to apophaticism, or the erasure, crossing out, or reversing the direction of affirmative theology. God is *not* good or wise or beautiful or loving or powerful in the way we, as humans, understand these attributes, predicated of a presumed subject they qualify. The closer we come to naming the reality that is God, the more the impotence of our ordinary language to speak of God is in evidence. That which is said, then, must always and immediately be unsaid. He shows this in *The Divine Names*:

> The indefiniteness beyond being
>   lies beyond beings.
> The unity beyond intellect
>   lies beyond intellect.
> The one beyond thought is
> unintelligible to all thinking.
> The good beyond logos:
> ineffable to all logos
> unity unifying every unity
> being beyond being
> non-intelligible intellect
> ineffable logos

27 Rolt, *Dionysius the Areopagite*, 95–96.

non-rationality
non-intelligibility
non-nameability
be-ing according to no being
cause of *being* to all; but itself: non-be-ing,
as it is beyond every being, and
So that it would properly and knowingly
manifest itself about itself.[28]

Dionysius's writing is frustratingly provocative in its reversals, denials, contradictions, paradoxes and oxymorons; it is a model itself of apophatic rhetoric. In chapter VII of *The Divine Names* he tells the reader that "it is necessary for us to investigate how we know God, which is neither intelligible, sensible, nor in general some being among beings." And then he offers this apophatic performance:

God is known
    through knowledge, and
    through unknowing.

Of God there is
    intellect, reason, knowledge,
    contact, sensation, opinion, imagination, name, and
    everything else.

God is
    not known, not spoken, not named,
    not something among beings, and
    not known in something among beings.

God is
    all in all,
    nothing in none,
    known to all in reference to all,
    known to no one in reference to nothing.
                For we say all of this correctly about God
                who is celebrated according
                to the analogy of all,
                of which it is the cause.[29]

St. Augustine, too, had puzzled: "Have I spoken or announced anything worthy of God? Rather I feel that I have done nothing but wish to

28. Dionysius, in Franke, *On What Cannot Be Said,* 163.
29. Ibid., 171.

speak: if I have spoken, I have not said what I wished to say. Whence do I know this, except because God is ineffable? If what I said were ineffable, it would not be said. And for this reason God should not be said to be ineffable, for when this is said something is said. And a contradiction in terms is created, since if that is ineffable which cannot be spoken, then that is not ineffable which can be called ineffable. This contradiction is to be passed over in silence rather than resolved verbally."[30]

Apophasis, explains William Franke, "can actually be apprehended only in discourse—in language insofar as it negates itself and tends to disappear as language . . . [A]pophatic discourses consist in words that negate themselves in order to evoke what is beyond words—and indeed beyond the limits of language altogether."[31] And Dionysius confirms this in *Divine Names*: "We leave behind us all our own notions of the divine. We call a halt to the activities of our minds and, to the extent that is proper, we approach the ray which transcends being. Here, in a manner no words can describe, preexisted all the goals of all knowledge and it is of a kind that neither intelligence nor speech can lay hold of it . . ."[32]

In the fourth and fifth chapters of his *Mystical Theology*, the author traces an ascending hierarchy of denials, denials of all the names of God— from the lowest "perceptual" names ("rock, "light"), derived as metaphors from material objects, to the highest "conceptual" names ("wisdom," "goodness," "beauty," "existence")—all negated one by one as he progresses up the scale, or ladder, of language until, ultimately, silence.

> Ascending higher we say:
> It is
>   not soul, not intellect
>   not imagination, opinion, reason and not understanding,
>   not logos, not intellection,
>   not spoken, not thought,
>   not number, not order,
>   not greatness, not smallness,
>   not equality, not inequality,
>   not likeness, not unlikeness,
>   not having stood, not moved, not at rest,
>   not powerful, not power,
>   not light,
>   not living, not life,
>   not being,

30. Augustine, *On Christian Doctrine*, 1:6.
31. Franke, *On What Cannot Be Said*, 1.
32. Dionysius, in ibid., 160.

not eternity, not time.
not intellectual contact with it,
not knowledge, not truth,
not king, not wisdom,
not one, not unity,
not divinity,
not goodness,
not spirit (as we know spirit),
not sonhood, not fatherhood,
not something other [than that] which is known
        by us or some other beings,
not something among what is not,
not something among what is,
not known as it is by beings,
not a knower of beings as they are:
There is neither logos, name, or knowledge of it.
It is not dark nor light,
        not error, and not truth.
There is universally
        neither position nor denial of it.
While there are produced positions and denials
of those after it,
we neither position nor deny it.

Since,
beyond all position is
        the all-complete and single cause of all;
        beyond all negation:
                the preeminence of that
                absolutely absolved from all
                and beyond the whole.[33]

Similarly with respect to movement and steps on a journey, St. John declares:

Thus, if it is true—and indeed it is—that the soul must journey by knowing God through what he is not rather than what he is, it must journey . . . by way of the denial and rejection of natural and supernatural apprehensions . . . God cannot be encompassed by any form or distinct knowledge.[34]

33. Dionysius, in ibid., 179–80.
34. Kavanaugh and Rodrigues, *Complete Works*, 268–69.

And just as the *Cloud* author, as we shall shortly see, will maintain the cataphatic basis of negative theology—its anchoring in the corporeal liturgical and devotional life and language of the monastery which is then "transcended" through a "forgetting"—apophatic theology proceeds by making affirmative statements that are then "un-said" in an ever-regressive movement. Yet "this movement," argues Gabriel Rochell in "Apophatic Preaching and the Postmodern Mind," "leaves traces in the mind of the hearer that become contemplative clues to the experience of God."[35]

For Dionysius, true speaking about God is a speaking that strikes human language dumb, speech linguistically taxed to the point of excess or exhaustion, and therein is its inadequacy—its "spiritual deserts," "silences," and "dark nights." It is language deployed to realize the language-defeating reality of the divine. "If talk about God is deficient," says Denys Turner, "this is a discovery made within the extending of it into superfluity, into that excess in which it collapses under its own weight . . . [T]he silence which falls in the embarrassment of prolixity is transformed into awe."[36] Negative theology, then, *affirms* a not-knowing, a silence; it is a "language of unsaying,"[37] or a "self-subverting utterance."[38] Silence here, or the refusal of discursive reflection, is a form of communication, wherein something is known at the somatic level. Likewise, for St. John the joy of encountering God is itself unspeakable—he is "unable to express the plenitude of [its] meaning in ordinary words."[39] Just as Plato's newly released prisoner at first faces the blinding intensity of light, what St. John first feels as absence is, rather, a resounding and almost unbearable fullness of meaning. As our ordinary language approaches the mystery of divine reality, one writer puts it, "it begins to break up and enter a new mode. Ordinary speech becomes extraordinary poetry, and extraordinary poetry shifts to exquisite music, and music in turn gives way to breathtaking design until a 'silent' word becomes the only adequate name for God."[40] In the *Spiritual Canticle* St. John had maintained:

> In contemplation God teaches the soul very quietly and secretly, without its knowing how, without the sound of words, and without the help of any bodily or spiritual faculty, in silence

35. Rochelle, "Apophatic Preaching," 411.

36. Davies and Turner, *Silence and the Word*, 18.

37. Ibid., 23.

38. Turner, *Darkness of God*, 21.

39. Kavanaugh and Rodrigues, *Complete Works*, 462.

40. Garcia-Rivera, "On a New List of Aesthetic Categories," 170.

and quietude . . . Some spiritual persons call this contemplation knowing by unknowing.[41]

This denial of all nameable divine essentiality will be central to contemporary philosopher Jean-Luc Marion's thinking, and to our sense of a theological aesthetics in Viola's work, founded on an analogy between aesthetic experience and that of revelation—a new sense of Beauty that reveals something beyond our experience and unites us to that revelation, or intimation of the sublime beneath the material surface of observable phenomena.

The Cloud of Unknowing

Another of the medieval thinkers consistently invoked by Viola is the anonymous author of *The Cloud of Unknowing*, a practical spiritual guidebook believed to have been written in the latter half of the 14th century by an English monk who counsels his young student to seek God not through knowledge but through affectivity, what he calls a "naked blind feeling of being"—a directly experiential mysticism no longer beholden to the "intellectual exercise and dialectical discipline that had generally characterized negative theologies since ancient Greece."[42] The Cloud author urges his disciple to negate all cognitive activity, an active effort of denial and unknowing which allows for the irruption of grace into the ordinary.[43] Cheryl Taylor has compellingly theorized this notion of transcendence within the context of *liminality*, a condition of open-ended betweenness—that is, between the traditional dualism of the active and contemplative lives, a space of "potential,"[44] and what, in the postmodern arena, Luce Irigaray has theorized as *intervalle*, a liminal identity which is the place or possibility of the divine—a "sensible transcendental" she calls it.[45] This sense of *transitus* in liminality, the passing into a state of being that cannot truly be materially depicted, only perceived or experienced—or rather, believed, held in mind or faith—is often invoked by Viola himself in the allusive words used in the titles of some of his works such as "Crossing," "Passing," "Surrender," "Unspoken," etc. In this way the subject, rendered "naked," is stripped of the familiar, of the stable and the normative, and is placed in a transitional or

---

41. Kavanaugh and Rodrigues, *Complete Works*, 626.
42. Franke, *On What Cannot Be Said*, 333.
43. See Turner, *Darkness of God*, chapter 8.
44. Taylor, "*Cloud* Texts," 145.
45. Berry and Wernick, *Shadow of Spirit*, 250.

liminal space, challenged and then transformed by the very impress of the unfamiliar. In this fissured subjectivity the subject is a *self-in-process*, open to the functioning of grace within the soul.[46] The *Cloud* Author counsels of this process:

> For when you first begin to undertake it, all that you find is a darkness, a sort of cloud of unknowing . . . This darkness and cloud is always between you and your God . . . and it prevents you from seeing him clearly by the light of understanding in your reason . . . When I say "darkness," I mean a privation of knowing.[47]

And again further on:

> Try as you might, this darkness and this cloud will remain between you and your God. You will feel frustrated, for your mind will be unable to grasp him, and your heart will not relish the delight of his love. But learn to be at home in this darkness.[48]

This metaphor of darkness or obscurity converges with Scripture in the Exodus story of Moses' encounter with God "in a dark cloud" on Mount Sinai (Exodus 20:21). In these meanings, faith is the darkness of un/non-knowing, the stripping away of material elements that hamper apprehension of the divine. Dark knowledge is dark in the sense that it is not a conceptual—enlightened—knowledge; St. John's Bride refers to it as an "I-don't-know-what" since it is not understandable, it is indescribable, unspeakable, a "primordial knowing."[49] This process of privation or renunciation of the attachments of the self to the self's own operations and its objects is dark because it removes from us our foundations of familiar comfort and sources of fulfillment, and transplants us into blinding nothingness—again the feeling of abandonment or "powerlessness" as St. John describes it.

The *Cloud of Unknowing*, with its central metaphors of negativity and hiddenness, draws on the mystical tradition of Pseudo-Dionysius—of whom, in fact, the Cloud author writes "Anyone who reads Denis' book

46. Maika J. Will draws a distinction in the agency of grace—God or man—between the Pseudo-Dionysius and the *Cloud* author: "the Areopagite suggests that the soul is given the grace to raise itself up to the transcendent God, while the *Cloud* author maintains instead that the transcendent God descends into the soul to work there directly through operant grace" (Will, "Dionysian Neoplatonism," 189; see also part two of this study, in the June 1992 issue).

47. Griffin, *Cloud of Unknowing*, 10–11, 17.

48. Franke, *On What Cannot Be Said*, 336.

49. The term "primordial knowing" is used by Larry Cooley in his article "Way to Ultimate Meaning."

will find confirmed there all that I have been trying to teach in this book from start to finish"—which has inspired generations of mystical searchers including John of the Cross. It draws also on the 14th-century Dominican philosopher-preacher Meister Eckhart, whose mystical speculations are grounded in linguistic opaqueness and paradox, in unusual metaphors and neologisms, in order to provoke unknowing through the very demonstration of language's inadequacies. Eckhart, argues William Franke, "brings to its full maturity the apophatic theological speculation of the Christian Middle Ages" and "makes peculiarly palpable the fundamental transformation of apophasis in a direction that has sometimes been conceptualized as a species of Christian existentialism."[50] In Sermon 83, Eckhart advises:

> So be silent, and do not chatter about God; for when you do chatter about him, you are telling lies and sinning . . . And do not try to understand God, for God is beyond all understanding . . . If you can understand anything about him, it in no way belongs to him, and insofar as you understand anything about him, that brings you into incomprehension, and from incomprehension you arrive at a brute's stupidity . . . So if you do not wish to be brutish, do not understand God who is beyond words . . . You should love him as he is a nonGod, a nonspirit, a nonperson, a nonimage, but as he is a pure, unmixed, bright "One," separated from all duality; and in that One we should eternally sink down, out of "something" into "nothing."[51]

Eckhart's very language is saturated with tropes of "nothingness," "emptiness," and "abyss," and steeped in images of stepping outside the self.[52] His sermons are expressive events charged with the sublime. "Negative theology," as least as Eckhart practices it, "is not just metaphysical speculation but is lived out in the diverse spheres of intellection, connotation, emotion, and sensation." Franke elaborates:

> On the basis of this new valorization of the existential world as inhabited by and answering to an unspeakable absolute, one that had become no longer a detached principle or indifferent origin but was infinitely active and present in conscious life, the later Middle Ages and Renaissance were to develop a broader understanding of spirit as the element in which what cannot be said or grasped or mastered by any human faculty is nevertheless

50. Franke, *On What Cannot Be Said*, 27.

51. Eckhart in Franke, *On What Cannot Be Said,* 295–97.

52. Viola speaks about reading Eckhart's sermons during his own self-isolating retreats to read and write. See Ross, *Bill Viola*, 145.

encountered and experienced, so as to become effectual in every human act and apprehension.[53]

It is Eckhart, in fact, who, we might speculate, can be credited as a principle driving force in the contemporary, postmodern, revival of apophaticism. The Dominican monk, preacher, and master teacher of theology in Paris, in his rhetorically and theologically confrontational sermons essentially invents a language that tests the very limits of language: "his daring neologisms, his peculiar employment of negative particles and prepositions, and his apophatic strategies of hyperbole, paradox, antithesis, and chiasmus . . . repeat but dialectically reverse[s] the order of a verbal sequence."[54] And through this rhetorical strategy he, like apophatics before him and like postmodern thinkers after, develop the theme of God as a Being that is beyond all limits of identity, Being opposed to any finite determination of being. Eckhart himself explains:

> That which is above every name excludes no name, but universally includes all names and in an equally indistinct way. None of these names will, consequently, be proper to it, save that which is above every name and is common to all names. But existence is common to all beings and names, and hence existence is the proper name of God alone.[55]

Thus, unnameabilty in Eckhart is not simply asserted as theory or theology—negative in the sense that it denies that the transcendent can be named or given attributes—but it is *performed*, in a continuous chain of denials and retractions in an endless chain of signifiers, as postmoderns will have it, and as Michael Sells argues "a propositionally unstable and dynamic discourse in which no single statement can rest on its own as true or false, or even as meaningful."[56]

Eckhart, then, preached the experience of God through the detachment from all objectified being, beyond language, beyond concept, eternal and outside time. St. John, too, had spoken of the negation—the poverty, nakedness, void—of the dark night as theological communication itself, in the sense of the emptying of the self transformed into the fullness of God. And that divine abyss was, for Eckhart, the hidden source from which all proceeds and to which all returns. Both men speak of an "interiority" wherein the self "detaches" from the world, moves "inward" to itself, and

53. Franke, *On What Cannot Be Said*, 28.
54. Ibid., 286.
55. Ibid., 287–88.
56. Sells, *Mystical Languages of Unsaying*, 3.

then "upward" to its source of Truth (God), liberating that self from the limitedness of the corporeal and emptying the self of self-will. By going inward, one escapes; that is the very imagery of Bill Viola's *Room for St. John of the Cross.* The dual images of "inwardness" and "ascent" are consistent in the theorizing of detachment as a dispossession or dismantling of selfhood, a human groping up toward the Wholly Other, to be formed again by God, who meets us in gracious self-revelation.[57] According to Eckhart, we must abandon the picture we have of God, let go of God as property or possession—hence the monk's infamous prayer: "Therefore pray God that we may be free of God." Every speaking, every image, every concept is insufficient. Human language and its conceptual apparatus are surpassed and affirm a not-knowing and a silence (a *not-* or *un-*saying). The absolute ineffability of God provides the motive for the bewildering and paradoxical ways in which Eckhart speaks about divine nature.[58] His is a rhetoric designed to induce—through its refusal of stability, ultimacy, and coherence—the unknowing and the dispersal of meaning, a tendency not lost on Derrida and other postmodern theologies.

Moreover, Eckhart's disorienting discourse has been characterized as Christianity with a Zen outlook, particularly in its emphasis on the process of emptying the self of self-will in order to recognize that union with God as already existing in the soul. This connection would not have been lost on Viola who early on in his career turned to close study of Eastern enlightenment philosophy and spiritual engagement from Buddhism to Sufi mysticism.[59] In fact, it was through the study and practice of Zen meditation that Viola first became aware of Eckhart and John of the Cross: "After moving away from my Christian upbringing," recounts Viola, "I got interested in Eastern culture, and I went to Japan, and I was practicing Zen meditation . . . They [Zen scholar Daisetz Suzuki and Sri Lankan art historian Ananda Coomaraswamy] began writing about people I was not familiar with, such as Meister Eckhart, St. John of the Cross, Hildegard von Bingen, and Plotinus, as well as Plato and Aristotle. They recognized these people . . . as part of the other side of the Western tradition, a tradition that was carried on in

---

57. Turner draws a greater distinction between the two mystics in his *Darkness of God* (chapter 7); there he also makes the point that the *Cloud* author is much more critical of the spatial metaphors of this descriptive language ("above," "below," "within," "without"); see 204–5.

58. See Colledge and McGinn, *Meister Eckhart: The Essential Sermons.*

59. Elizabeth ten Grotenhuis has written eloquently about these East-West connections for Viola in her essay "Something Rich and Strange: Bill Viola's Uses of Asian Spirituality," in Townsend, *Art of Bill Viola,* 161–79.

the East and developed well beyond the advent of rational positivist thinking (which took over in the West) and right up into the twentieth century."[60]

Finally, this "deconstructive" activity in language signals the disable-
ment of the intellect, as Denys Turner argues, in the same sense, I will
show, that makes operative and relevant the encounter with the *sublime*.
Apophaticism simply shows, Turner writes, "that God cannot be known
intellectually. The clutter of intellect and language being cleared away, room
is left in a darkness of the consequent *intellectual* unknowing; and there it
is love which yields a direct experience of God unmediated by any work of
thought or intellect."[61] But while the negative theologian and the deconstruc-
tivist share a similar interest in that which escapes total description, mystical language and its imagery, I think, retain the *gesture* beyond themselves
into the realm of unmediated wisdom in the sublime and the transcendental
signified.[62] That is to say, there is *something* that is unsayable; we know from
faith it is not a nothing, an absence. It is, in fact, as Derrida himself called it
in *Languages of the Unsayable*, "the language of promise," or, perhaps better
I would posit, a language of *hope*, situated in the midst of promise, of the
not-yet or the *unfinished*, and in hope, trust and openness to infinite and
overwhelming possibilities. And so it is to the Sublime that we now turn.

60. Ibid., 162. Interestingly, Viola's *Room for St. John of the Cross* was recently re-
assembled and on view in the exhibition at the Guggenheim Museum in New York,
The Third Mind: American Artists Contemplate Asia. It is also important to note cross-
cultural approaches to apophatic traditions, such as Williams, *Denying Divinity*, and
Scharfstein, *Ineffability*.

61. Turner, "Art of Unknowing," 484.

62. On the use of the term "transcendental signified," see Pokorn, "Language and
Discourse of the Cloud of Unknowing," 408–21.

3

In Excess

Towards a Theological Sublime

Such knowledge is too wonderful for me;
it is too high, I cannot attain to it.

—PSALM 139:6

SUBLIMITY, A CONCEPT FIRST presented in an aesthetic treatise attrib-
uted to the first-century Greek rhetorician, literary scholar and philosopher Longinus, is, in short, about the power of descriptive failure,
about the defeat of expressible thought or articulable sensation, and the
inherent richness in that inability to apprehend; the sublime, in other
words, as a disruptive force marks the limits of reason with an intimation of what might lie beyond those limits.[1] This is the paradox of
the sublime, mindfulness of an unbridgeable gap between the world of
sensuous reality and the realm of the supersensible—made available to
reason by that very failure of reason. As Slavoj Žižek explains:

> This is also why an object evoking in us the feeling of Sublim-
> ity gives us simultaneously pleasure and displeasure: it gives us
> displeasure because of its inadequacy to the Thing-Idea [the
> supersensible Idea], but precisely through this inadequacy it

1. For a good, succinct historical overview of the concept of the Sublime, see Shaw,
Sublime.

36

gives us pleasure by indicating the true, incomparable greatness of the Thing, surpassing every possible phenomenal, empirical experience.[2]

Architects of the Sublime

For Immanuel Kant, arch-theorist of the Enlightenment, the sublime—centerpiece to his *Critique of Judgement* (1790)—describes that experience which reveals to the mind Nature's power to suggest to the imagination, to intimate and embody, what is visually unrepresentable. In the presence of the sublime—denoted, as Kant had it, by vast and powerful objects and overwhelming spaces—we are reminded that Nature as boundless manifold is not ours to know completely; the imagination cannot grasp it in a single clarifying image, nor can understanding deal with it—a defect of or affront to human faculties unacceptable under an *a priori* law of reason which demands wholeness of comprehension.

This experience, characterized by Kant as the *mathematical sublime*—vastness of scale, that which is great in spatial extension—and the *dynamical sublime*—great power, force and energy in Nature—is such that our perceptual faculties, rendered incapable of taking in the sheer immensity of Nature's manifold, are overwhelmed, resulting in an estimation of power which de-centers the viewer into an awareness of his own trifling position in the universe—what philosopher Paul Crowther has aptly called "existential vertigo."[3] The view, in our immediate perceptual estimation of it, seems a limitless phenomenal mass, utterly unfathomable, and as such the imagination is launched into vain effort to comprehend its magnitude in such a way that leads to the question of the indeterminate (unrepresentable) idea of the infinite. Thus for Kant the sublime is not something "out there" in the world; it is, rather, "the cast of mind in appreciating it that we have to estimate as sublime."[4] This marking of the limit of the rational mind will be echoed in postmodern rehabilitations of the sublime, as for instance in Jean-François Lyotard for whom the work of art could prompt the breakdown of our conceptual system and who declared, "There are no sublime objects, but only sublime feelings."[5]

2. Žižek, *Sublime Object*, 229.
3. Crowther, *Kantian Sublime*, 171.
4. Kant, *Critique of Judgement*, in Davies and Turner, *Silence and the Word*, 106.
5. Lyotard, "Presenting the Unpresentable," 65.

In short, Kant construes the sublime as occasioned by powers that transcend the phenomenal self and prompt a mode of awe or reverence. The sublime is that which, through the suggestion of perceptually, imaginatively, or emotionally overwhelming properties, succeeds in rendering the scope (and limit) of some human capacity vivid to the senses and opens up a space for encounter with the *noumenon*. He points here to a break between two dimensions of reality—the phenomenal and the noumenal. The sublime, according to Kant, is in effect our way of experiencing our own limits vis-à-vis the unknown, but an unknown (God) we can relate to.

For Kant the material limit to our perceptual and rational capacity serves as a kind of *analogue* of total understanding; that is to say, we can never *know* the infinite, but we can imagine it, think it as an idea, and thus experience the consolation that something transcends the limitations of our phenomenal being—thus for Kant preserving a sense of mind's superior ability to transcend some vast physicality or infinite power over something so challenging. In his earlier *Critique of Practical Reason* (1788), he sets this up:

> Two things fill the mind with ever new and increasing admiration and reverence, the more often and more steadily one reflects upon them: the starry heavens above me and the moral law within me . . . The first view of a countless multitude of worlds annihilates, as it were, my importance as an animal creature . . . The second, on the contrary, infinitely raises my worth as an intelligence by my personality, in which the moral law reveals to me a life independent of animality and even of the whole sensible world.[6]

That initial experience of the disproportion between the mind's ordering power and an ungraspable complexity, thus, may serve us as an analogue for another situation, one in which we attempt to comprehend something beyond the scope of our understanding—when we find ourselves attempting, for instance, to grasp (to describe and to know) such ideas as God and the Infinite. For Kant, we can never grasp the whole "beyond" this world, limited as we are in the human situation of being in the world; we don't have access to its ultimate Absoluteness. But, as with the sublime, our self-conscious awareness of perceptual and rational limitations is what allows for the reassuring intimation that something transcends finite being. As St. John of the Cross had put it: "This sublime knowledge" which "transcends what is naturally attainable . . . consists in a certain touch of the divinity produced in the soul, and thus it is God himself who is expressed and tasted

6. Kant, *Critique of Practical Reason*, in Costelloe, *The Sublime*, 48.

there."[7] In encountering our rational and linguistic limits, we may abandon our pretentions to *knowledge* of God. As Denys Turner eloquently glosses the issue in *The Darkness of God*:

> Is it not better to say, as expressive of the apophatic, simply that God is what is on the other side of anything at all we can be conscious of, whether of its presence or of its absence? . . . [W]e can, in a sense, be aware of God, even be 'conscious' of God; but only in that sense in which we can be conscious of the *failure* of our knowledge, not knowing what it is that our knowledge fails to reach.[8]

Of course, the sublime as aesthetic category has its own considerable tradition, a tradition not unknown to Viola. Seventeenth-century essayist and poet Joseph Addison, in an essay titled "The Pleasure of the Imagination," published in *The Spectator* in 1712, described this freedom from perceptual confinement in our experiences of the sublime as that which resists the mind's call to order:

> Our imagination loves to . . . grasp at anything that is too big for its capacity. We are flung into a pleasing astonishment at such unbounded views, and feel a delightful . . . amazement in the soul at the apprehension of them. The mind of man naturally hates everything that looks like a restraint upon it, and is apt to fancy itself under a sort of confinement . . .[9]

Our ideas of the sublime, according to Addison, are rooted in sense perceptions; the greatness of the sublime, however, is not an inherent quality of nature (storms, earthquakes, disasters) or in the object of its source; rather, it is an act of reflection or mode of consciousness that surpasses the capacity of imagination to contain.

Similarly, 18th-century philosopher Edmund Burke, in his 1756 treatise *A Philosophical Inquiry into the Origin of Our Ideas of the Sublime and the Beautiful*, situates the quality of fear and attraction in the sublime, particularly in a psychological calculus of pleasure and pain, both inviting and fearsome, which relies on a more strongly empirical sense of bodily orientation and an experience that "pierces" us to "our inaccessible and inmost parts":

---

7. Kavanaugh and Rodrigues, *Complete Works*, 246–47.

8. Turner, *Darkness of God*, 264–65.

9. Addison, *Collected Works*, III, 397–98.

> Whatever is fitted in any sort to excite the ideas of pain, and danger, that is to say, whatever is in any sort terrible, or is conversant about terrible objects, or operates in a manner analogous to terror, is a source of the Sublime; that is, it is productive of the strongest emotion which the mind is capable of feeling.[10]

And this is not altogether unlike an understanding of the body for John of the Cross, for whom in order to acquire supreme knowledge, God must "begin by touching the low state and the extremes of the senses. And from there he must gradually bring the soul after its own manner to the other end, spiritual wisdom, which is incomprehensible to the senses."[11] For both Burke and St. John, a mode of pleasure derives from the alienating experience of danger or pain. And, in one of his few references to the Divine, Burke goes further to posit that the mind is so "struck with [God's] power" as to "shrink into the minuteness of [its] own nature and [is], in a manner, annihilated before him."[12]

Burke is in agreement with Kant (and Addison before him) that the sublime is a source of pleasure, albeit of a negative sort, and that it is an attribute not of nature but rather of the mind. Kant, however, shifts the emphasis from the realm of the physiological—in Burke's sense of pleasure derived from self-preservation and security in the face of terror ("Terror is a passion which always produces delight when it does not press too closely")—and onto the grander plane of the transcendental.

That the sublime came to be thus characterized by the experience of transcendence and ineffability is observed by Rudolf Otto in his seminal 1913 study, *The Idea of the Holy*, in which he makes the perhaps more Romantic[13] association between the sublime and the numinous:

> While the element of "dread" is gradually overborne, the connexion of "the sublime" and "the holy" becomes firmly established as a legitimate schematization and is carried on into the highest forms of religious consciousness—a proof that there exists a hidden kinship between the numinous and the sublime which is something more than accidental analogy, and to which Kant's *Critique of Judgement* bears distant witness.[14]

10. Burke, *Philosophical Inquiry*, 33.

11. Kavanaugh and Rodrigues, *Complete Works*, 206.

12. Burke, *Philosophical Inquiry*, 57.

13. In this context see also Ian Greig's essay "Quantum Romanticism" in Hoffman and Whyte, *Beyond the Finite*, 106–127.

14. Quoted in Ward, *Theology and Contemporary Critical Theory*, 126.

Recalling our 16th-century mystics, the "*mysterium tremendum*" for Otto, that overpowering absolute before which we are sorely aware of our own creatureliness, "may burst in sudden eruption up from the depths of the soul with spasms and convulsions, or lead to the strangest excitements, to intoxicated frenzy, to transport, and to ecstasy . . . It may become the hushed, trembling, and speechless humility of the creature in the presence of—whom or what? In the presence of that which is a mystery inexpressible and above all creatures."[15]

Burke is of further relevance to our study here in his locating the sublime in states of emptiness and privation, in darkness, solitude and silence: "to make anything very terrible, obscurity seems in general to be necessary . . . Everyone will be sensible of this, who considers how greatly night adds to our dread."[16] This echoes the sense of spiritual loss initially described by John of the Cross, who spoke of the "obscurity" of faith and its "dark night," which seems to do away with all discursive knowledge, acts, ideas and images. Such obscurity of faith for St. John impresses on the mind that the intellect can neither, through its own power, fully acquire the kind of knowledge that faith affords nor fully understand the content of faith once revealed. "To reach union with the wisdom of God, he writes in *The Ascent of Mount Carmel*, "a person must advance by unknowing rather than by knowing."[17] And again:

> Other knowledge is acquired by the light of the intellect, but not the knowledge of faith . . . How wonderful it was. A cloud, dark in itself, could illuminate the night . . . faith, a dark and obscure cloud to souls (also a night in that it blinds and deprives them of their natural light), illumines and pours light into their darkness by means of its own darkness.[18]

It is tempting here, and not without relevance, to consider Friedrich Nietzsche's account of the "Dionysian" aspect of art in relation to the sublime as sketched above. Indeed, Kant scholar Paul Guyer argues the case for us: "if we take the Dionysian as Nietzsche's version of the sublime, then Nietzsche has radically reconceived the experience of the sublime as an intimation of the fundamental nonrationality of existence, rather than its rationality . . ."[19] In a remarkable echo of St. John on the redemptive release from suffering in transcendence of the self, Nietzsche writes in the *Birth*

15. Otto, *Idea of the Holy*, 1–3.

16. Burke, *Philosophical Inquiry*, 59.

17. Kavanaugh and Rodrigues, *Complete Works*, 126.

18. Ibid., 158.

19. Costelloe, *Sublime*, 115.

of Tragedy: ". . . with sublime gestures he shows us that the whole world of agony is needed in order to compel the individual to generate the releasing and redemptive vision and then, lost in contemplation of that vision, to sit calmly in his rocking boat in the midst of the sea."[20]

Returning here to Kant, in our vain attempt to comprehend infinity, imagination's inadequacy is first experienced as frustration (disequilibrium, suffering, pain), but then gives way to *pleasure* arising from our awareness that this inadequacy exemplifies the limits of our perceptual ability. Echoing Burke, Kant writes in the *Critique of Judgement*:

> The feeling of the sublime is . . . at once a feeling of displeasure, arising from the inadequacy of imagination in the aesthetic estimation of magnitude to attain to its estimation by reason, and a simultaneously awakened pleasure, arising from this very judgement of the inadequacy of the . . . faculty of sense being in accord with reason . . .[21]

Kant's division between the phenomenal and noumenal, or the sensible and the supersenible, further extends to the human self. On the one hand, we are embodied creatures of feeling and sensibility, who think and act in time and space. This means that as phenomenal beings we are part of nature and are subject to determination by nature's causal laws. On the other hand, in so far as it is the human subject that imposes this framework through the categories of the understanding—the forms of intuition (spatio-temporality, causality)—the ultimate self must in some sense be presumed to lie beyond the phenomenal world. It must, in other words, be a noumenal or supersensible self. Thus, as Paul Crowther argues, Kant "gives the supersensible self a negative characterization—namely as that aspect of the self which is not in space and time, and not subject to the categories."[22]

Henri Bergson and an Excursus on Time

The early modern philosophy of Henri Bergson offers a possible point of intervention in thinking about the sublime, particularly with respect to Viola's treatment of extended perception (what Bergson has called "psychological time"[23]), as time is a crucial element in what initiates the sublime in his work, work that requires patience, attention, and slowing down. Viola

20. Nietzsche, *Birth of Tragedy*, in Costelloe, *Sublime*, 117.

21. Kant, *Critique of Judgement*, §27.

22. Crowther, *Kantian Sublime*, 17.

23. Bergson, *Introduction to Metaphysics*, 214.

speaks of the "preciousness of time," something that perhaps today more than ever, as "needing our attention."[24]

Central to Bergson's thinking is the primordiality of experiential time in consciousness: conscious states understood, not, in the mathematical, scientific notion of time, as a sequence of successive, atomistic, and discrete moments—the time of clocks—but as a multiplicity continually unfolding in "duration." The order or organization of conscious states, on this view, does not correspond exactly with the order of things in a material—that is, spatial, system. These units distort rather than reflect our inner (subjective) experience of time; they serve the practical conception of time that regulates society, but are inadequate as symbols of felt experience. Duration of reality, for Bergson, is an indivisible "flow" which the intellect, for practical purposes of manipulation and control, separates into definable and rationally manageable pieces; it does this by translating time into a logical system of stable concepts, into space.

In his 1889 *Essai sur les donnés immédiates de la conscience*—literally "Essay on what is immediately given in consciousness" (a more accurate description of his main concerns, but translated into English as *Time and Free Will*)—Bergson defined reality as an indivisible pervasive continuity of time. Here Bergson described the temporal dimension of human consciousness as synonymous with creative freedom; in fact, in seeking an alternative to the limitations of scientific knowledge, he urged artists to free themselves from the spatiality of external objects in order to depict reality. This essay, argues Suzanne Guerlac, launches a powerful critique of Kant: "Bergson will attempt to draw a critical line, not between phenomena and noumena, as Kant had done, but between the living and the inert. Whereas inert things are the appropriate objects of science, Bergson believed that living beings, states of consciousness . . . can only be known through a metaphysical method he will call intuition."[25] A succession of conscious states must not be interpreted, as is the inveterate habit of mind, Bergson insisted, as an order of states in space—the phenomenal order of experience is not itself a spatial order. The enduring reality of changing conscious states—indivisible continuous consciousness—is absolutely different from a reality extended in space (and Bergson saw the artist as one who disentangles definite shapes from within that continuity of consciousness). Whereas entities in space are impenetrable, states of consciousness on Bergson's view "mutually penetrate each other" and are bound together in a relationship of enduring continuity—a ceaseless flow of thoughts, feelings, and perceptions. The successive

24. Interview, August 19, 2013.
25. Guerlac, *Thinking in Time*, 28.

and interpenetrative states of consciousness merge into one another, each retaining something of what has just passed and each giving intimation of what is to come—a fusion of the past with the present and the anticipated future. States of consciousness come and go and have their temporal meaning in a "duration" which is always *within* consciousness itself. In *An Introduction to Metaphysics* (1903), Bergson argued:

> There is . . . a continuous flux . . . a succession of states, each of which announces that which follows and contains that which precedes it. They can, properly speaking, only be said to form multiple states when I have already passed them and turn back to observe their track. Whilst I was experiencing them they were so solidly organized, so profoundly animated with a common life, that I could not have said where any one of them finished or where another commenced. In reality no one of them begins or ends, but all extend into each other.[26]

The external time with which we organize our ordinary experience in the world, in the spatial world of succession of points or "presents" is, the philosopher argued in *Time and Free Will*, something entirely incommensurate with this inner reality of "duration" as we experience it in conscious life. We can thus think of simultaneity as without spatial distinction.

> I cannot escape the objection that there is no state of mind, however simple, which does not change every moment, since there is no consciousness without memory, and no continuation of a state without the addition, to the present feeling, of the memory of past moments. It is this which constitutes duration. Inner duration is the continuous life of a memory which prolongs the past into the present, the present either containing within it a distinct form, the ceaselessly growing image of the past, or, more probably, showing by its continual change of quality the heavier and still heavier load we drag behind us as we grow older. Without this survival of the past into the present there would be no duration, but only instantaneity.[27]

It is this theme of memory that is of interest here—the multivalent and multidimensional nature of perception in time, and the notion of a temporal continuity connecting the remembered past to a dynamic present. Viola has himself often spoken of our "ability to extend the self into time with

---

26. Bergson, *Introduction to Metaphysics*, 9–10.
27. Ibid., 38.

the capacity to anticipate and recall."[28] Memory renders absence present, while keeping absence absent. The full apprehension of "duration," *la duree*, is possible only in memory wherein the past is accumulated in its fullness. Immediate sensory perception, then, is bound, for Bergson, with the creative forces of memory, where memory strengthens and enriches present perception. The interaction of no longer distinct "past" and "present" is defined as an indivisible movement and, as Gilles Deleuze has argued, as a simultaneity of differences marked by breaks;[29] moments or "instants" are markings abstracted from the flow of the plenum, from, as Bergson himself put it, "the plenitude of becoming."

Change is for Bergson a continuous process occurring within the conscious self in which "states" are not individually demarcated units, but mere points of greatest intensity trailing off indefinitely within the unbroken fabric of experience—a *becoming*, or poetic creation. Here is Bergson in his 1907 *Creative Evolution*, in which he specifies the constantly changing state of consciousness in terms of the perception of external objects.

> I say that I change, but the change seems to me to reside in the passage from one state to the next: of each state, taken separately I am apt to think that it remains the same, during all the time that it prevails. Nevertheless, a slight effort to attention would reveal to me that there is no feeling, no idea, no volition which is not undergoing change every moment: if a mental state ceased to vary, its duration would cease to flow. Let us take the most stable of internal states, the visual perception of a motionless external object. The object may remain the same, I may look at it from the same side, at the same angle, in the same light; nevertheless the vision I now have of it differs from that which I have just had, even if only because the one is an instant older than the other. My *memory is there which conveys something of the past into the present.* My mental state, as it advances on the road of time, is continually swelling with the duration which *it accumulates*: it goes on increasing . . . Still more is this the case with *states more deeply internal, such as sensations, feelings, desires, etc., which do not correspond, like a simple visual perception, to an unvarying external object.* But it is expedient to disregard this uninterrupted change, and to notice it only when it becomes sufficient to impress a new attitude on the body, a new direction of the attention. Then, and then only, we find that our state has

28. Viola, *Reasons for Knocking*, 278.

29. See Paul Douglass, "Deleuze's Bergson," in Burwick and Douglass, *Crisis in Modernism*, 368–88.

changed. The truth is that we change without ceasing, and that the state itself is nothing but change.[30]

Expressed here is the idea that that attention is malleable, susceptible to dissolution, fusions, forgetting, and recalling—a compounding of anticipation, recollection, and immediate experience. This is true to Viola's manipulations of time and has resonance in Bergson's notion of *la dureé* in perception and the multiplicity continually unfolding in the seamless flow of duration, incorporating the immanent past in the experiences of the present—what the philosopher refers to as *memory*. "Duration," Gilles Deleuze has summed up Bergson, "is essentially memory . . . the conservation *and* preservation of the past in the present."[31] He continues:

> The past and the present do not denote two successive movements, but two elements which cooexist. One is the present, which does not cease to pass, and the other is the past, which does not cease to be but through which all presents pass . . . each present goes back to itself as past.[32]

For Bergson, then, we mistakenly divide up the flow of real time into units of space, into "instants," which are the extensions of these units. That is, we convert the simultaneity of duration into abruptions of instants, and we do this because we have learned to "spatialize" time—this is the distinction between real, lived time and its "spatialization" or static conceptualization into objects, events, and activities of ordinary experience. Moreover, our conceptual thinking and its linguistic expression are "molded" upon this pre-prescribed world, a world "already made." Our intellect, in reflecting or confirming this world—"in professing to reconstruct reality with percepts and concepts whose function is to make it stationary"—only serves to obscure reality itself, that is, the world in real time or duration.

> Our mind, which seeks for solid points of support, has for its main function in the ordinary course of life that of representing states and things. It takes, at long intervals, almost instantaneous views of the undivided mobility of the real. It thus obtains sensations and ideas. In this way, it substitutes for the continuous the discontinuous, for motion stability, for tendency in process of change, fixed points marking a direction of change and tendency. This *substitution is necessary to common-sense, to*

---

30. Bergson, *Creative Evolution*, 1–2, my emphasis.

31. Deleuze, *Bergsonism*, 51.

32. Ibid., 59

language, to practical life, and even . . . to positive science . . . In that lies what we call exactitude and precision.[33]

On this view, while thought-in-language synthesizes the complex material of sensuous experience—its indeterminacy and ambiguity—into homogenous objective concepts, like standardized units adapted to social discourse, perception, by contrast, demands the wealth—the flexibility and extendability—of variable perception. Words "store up the stable, common and consequently impersonal element in the impressions of mankind," and "overwhelm or at least cover over the delicate and fugitive impressions of our individual consciousness."[34] This inability of language to describe duration actually reveals, for Bergson, the very nature of the limitations of our linguistic apparatus; as part of our intelligence, language is essentially a set of abstract signs whose task is to immobilize the experience of time, making the expression of change impossible. It is language, once again, that alienates us from direct experience. While language may be able to communicate the content of my experience in an intelligible way, the quality of what is being experienced is (linguistically) inexpressible; language, in effect, evacuates the multiplicity and mobility of the nuance, complexity and richness of the quality of that experience. To fix a name or word to something is to conceptualize experience and to lose sight of the deeper impression of innermost sensation:

> . . . the intuition of duration, when it is exposed to the rays of the understanding, in like manner quickly turns into fixed, distinct and immobile concepts. In the living mobility of things the understanding is bent on marking real or virtual stations, it notes departures and arrivals; for this is all that concerns the thought of man in so far as it is simply human. It is *more than human to grasp what is happening in the interval*. But philosophy can only be an effort to transcend the human condition.[35]

It is the subverting of the conventional signifying systems of verbal discourse that Julia Kristeva, in her *Revolution of Poetic Language*, assigns to poetry, ascribing it to the category of the "semiotic," a sort of fluid, pleasurable excess over precise, univocal meaning, which takes delight in destroying or negating the rigid signifying systems of the social-symbolic order.[36] It is this "pleasurable excess" St. John describes. Apophatic, like

33. Ibid., 65, my emphasis.
34. Bergson, *Essai*, 132.
35. Bergson, *Introduction to Metaphysics*, 65, my emphasis.
36. Kristeva, *Revolution in Poetic Language*.

poetic, discourse is propositionally unstable and dynamic, effecting a kind of ecstatic instability, liberated from logic, with effect on our perception. *Rupture* in language (the term is Kristeva's) occurs in the poetic text by pushing linguistic signification to its extreme limit—through, for instance, rhythm, intonation, sound-play, repetition—subverting stability, precision, and clarity in meaning, rendering it mobile, plural, and open to potentially new forms and disrupting fixed hearer/reader-subject positions.

> Indifferent to language . . . this space underlying the written is rhythmic, unfettered, irreducible to its intelligible verbal translation . . . What is more, when poetic language . . . transgresses grammatical rules, the positing of the symbolic finds itself subverted . . . as a possessor of meaning . . .[37]

If, then, Bergson's "duration" is a notion of time radically independent of space (and language), it is inaccessible to reflective consciousness, as cognitive thinking represents things in space—a form of symbolic representation. Duration can only be lived or experienced. There is much more at stake than the supposed "instant" of visual perception, if perception/experience is understood to be an extended—and lived—activity, one of continuous adjusting, shifting attention, forgetting, calling back into memory. And it is this sense of extendedness to perception that matters in Bergson's "*durée*."

There is a similar redefinition of time conveyed by our mystics' reversion to a pre-modern idea of non-linear, non-measurable time—an idea, according to Viola, captured by its artists as well: "artists in the early fifteenth century were not burdened by the idea of optical representation as being locked into a single moment of time, so they were able to show the same person in multiple places within the same landscape in a single picture."[38] He is drawing attention here to a very real distinction of orders of realty—that of ritual and that of narrative—that correspond to two opposing conceptions of time: *ritual time* (eternal recurrence) and *narrative time* (perpetual present). And this redefinition of the temporal is registered in his own art of duration and absorption—in slow motion, time lapse, accelerations and decelerations of time—that extend the moment of viewing into a time of attentiveness and receptivity, wherein what is captured is, in a sense, the *invisible*. "The invisible," Viola says, "is always much more present than the visible."[39] Linear and sequential (narrative) time is disrupted in the form of large, slow-moving, mesmerizing images that, the artist contends, "extend

---

37. Kristeva, *Kristeva Reader*, 97–132.
38. Walsh, *Bill Viola*, 212.
39. Viola in Townsend, *Art of Bill Viola*, 75.

the self into time with the capacity to anticipate and recall." Thinking in time, for Bergson, through its very iterative structure, "crushes duration."[40] As such, we are invited, by implication, to imagine a process "before" signification or coding, a "pre-linguistic" experience, and thus a shift from the (modernist) certainties of mechanism to the (postmodern) potentialities/anxieties of indeterminacy. These manipulations of temporal experience are suited to the technologies of time-based media, which therefore allow for a new consideration of the sublime in contemporary art.

Lyotard and the Apophatic Postmodern Sublime

For French philosopher, sociologist and literary theorist Jean-François Lyotard, the sublime (in art) is essential in our postmodern age, an age in which all legitimizing and stabilizing narratives have been shattered, as the sublime keeps relevant metaphysical thinking.[41]

> That which is not demonstrable is that which stems from Ideas . . . The universe is not demonstrable; neither is humanity, the end of history, the moment, the species, the good, the just, etc.— or, according to Kant, absolutes in general.[42]

Lyotard's *Lessons on the Analytic of the Sublime* (1991) is in many respects a renewal of Kant's critical project. Philosopher David Johnson explains:

> Following Kant very closely, Lyotard identifies the experience of sublimity as the simultaneous feeling of pleasure and pain that accompanies the imagination's inevitably failed attempt to present to thought an intuition that would adequately correspond to an idea of the absolute generated by the faculty of reason. Through this failure, thought is made to feel the unintuitable presence of this idea of the absolute, as well as the superiority of the faculty of reason over both the imagination and the phenomena of nature the latter presents. For Lyotard, the essential mechanism of this experience can thus be summarized in one short formula: the *presentation of the unpresentable* . . . It is this humbling failure of the imagination before reason, in spite of

---

40. Guerlac, *Thinking in Time*, 2.
41. Lyotard, "Presenting the Unpresentable," 64–69.
42. Ibid., 68.

the former's greatest efforts, that gives rise to the painful component of the feeling engendered in the sublime.[43]

According to Lyotard, contemporary art—abstract art, in particular, which for Lyotard representes a new apophaticism—can give new form to Kant's "negative presentation" of the unpresentable; it can make "ungraspable allusions to the invisible within the visible."[44] The incapacity of the imagination produces a negative presentation of what exceeds presentation, "a sign of the presence of the absolute." And Lyotard brings this to bear on modern art which will, he argues, "'present' something though negatively; it will therefore avoid figuration or representation."[45] Once again we find a denial of and collapse of the Logos, wherein "language enters into a generalized crisis and the currency of the word goes bust. The . . . collapse of verbal assurance fosters cultures that can be characterized as 'apophatic,' that is, as veering into widespread worries about the reliability of words and even into wholesale refusal of rational discourse."[46] "The aesthetic of the sublime," Lyotard argues elsewhere, "is where modern art . . . finds its impetus . . . showing that there is something we can conceive of which we can neither see nor show."[47] The "presence" he identifies as "a kind of transcendental pre-logic in which thought and sensation are complicit" is prior to an orientation by the categories of the understanding that enable feeling to be thought. This "presence" does not correspond to the ontological order of things in themselves, the immediate apprehension of which was for Lyotard, as for Kant, impossible. The presentation of the sublime, then, is negative; it is, Lyotard argues, "compatible with the formless," it exceeds the Kantian faculties of imagination—understanding and reason—and is thus freighted with negativity in words like "abyss," "unboundedness," "incommensurate," "unconditioned"; it is an awakening of the idea of the supersensible in the subjectivity of contemplation on the sublime. For Lyotard it acknowledges the "desire for the unknown" in the postmodern:

> The postmodern would be that which, in the modern, puts forward the unpresentable in presentation itself; that which denies the solace of good forms . . . that which searches for new presentations, not in order to enjoy them, but in order to impart a stronger sense of the unpresentable.[48]

43. Johnson, "The Postmodern Sublime," in Costelloe, *The Sublime*, 118–131, 120.
44. Ibid.
45. Ibid., 122.
46. Franke, *On What Cannot Be Said*, 9.
47. Lyotard, *The Postmodern Explained*, 9–10.
48. Quoted in Ward, *Theology and Contemporary Critical Theory*, 137–38.

This sense of the "unseen" is central to Bill Viola's work. Its appeal is, I want to call it, a *poetics of hope* in the as-yet-unsatisfied desire for union and fellowship with the (divine) other, such that the divine—God—is present in being hidden. We might also call it "desire," desire for that which is beyond experience, for the transcendent reality—the pleasurable excess—that can never be attained but only morally intuited—a desire for the Other. It is a God whose presence is felt—revealed—indirectly; and its givenness or grace rests upon our disinterestedness (in the Kantian sense of disinterest). It involves a *phenomenology of hope*, such that we remain receptively open to the overwhelming *promise* of the "appearance," or in the Christian understanding, "reappearance" of God.

4

The Unseen Passions and the Ethics of Sublimity

The responsibility for the other can not have begun in my commitment,
in my decision . . . The responsibility for the other is the locus in which is
situated the null-site of subjectivity . . . All my inwardness is invested in the
form of a despite-me, for-another. Despite-me, for-another is signification
par excellence.

—LEVINAS, *OTHERWISE THAN BEING
OR BEYOND ESSENCE*

WITHIN THE THEORETICAL FRAMEWORK of apophatic theology and the
philosophical sublime, I want now to return in a more concrete way
to Bill Viola's art and specifically to a much more recent series of installations collectively titled *The Passions*, a project organized and first
exhibited at the J. Paul Getty Museum in Los Angeles, which the artist
began in 2000 as a participating scholar in a year-long study sponsored
by the Getty Research Institute. The Getty's focus topic that year was
how to represent, in word and image, the power and complexity of human emotion. Viola's project takes the form of more than twenty video
pieces variously connected by the theme of extreme emotion, aimed
at conveying fundamental but inarticulate human states of being: love,
hope, sorrow, joy, desire. Here we do well to recall Henri Bergson on

the "terrorism" of the "brutal word"—language "which stores up what is stable, common, and therefore impersonal in human impressions." What suffers most at the hands of "the brutal word" are emotions, passions. Bergson in the passage quoted below is speaking of the *fires* of love, a vivid analogy very much at the core of St. John's poetry (and Viola's iconography) in which the 16th-century mystic referred to the real "heating and enkindling" force of "fire" that "transforms the wood into itself and makes it as beautiful as it is itself," this, the saint goes on, is like the "divine, loving fire of contemplation. Before transforming the soul, it purges it of all contrary qualities . . . For love is like a fire that always rises upward as though longing to be engulfed in its center."[1] Here, now, is Bergson:

> A violent love, a deep melancholy invades our soul, provoking a thousand diverse elements that melt together, interpenetrate, without definite contours, without the least tendency to separate themselves one from another. Their originality is at this cost. A moment ago each one of them borrowed an indefinable coloration from the milieu where it was placed. Now it is bleached out and ready to receive a name . . . Feeling is a living being, which develops, and is therefore always changing . . . when we separate these moments out, unfurling time into space, the feeling loses its animation and its color. Then we are left with only the shadow of ourselves.[2]

"Self-annihilation," Bill Viola had remarked in a similar context, "becomes a necessary means to transcendence and liberation."[3] This is perhaps best expressed, as a single piece, in his 1996 *The Crossing*, comprised of a two-sided screen projection, reminiscent of the color fields of a Rothko canvas. On one side (see Figure 4), a single man walking toward the viewer from a distance comes into view; he stops, then accompanied by a sound rising to a deafening roar, he is overcome by a rising sheet of flames (see Figure 5); on the other (see Figure 3), a slow drip of water becomes a deluge— images of immolation and inundation, the self-emptying of man, divine acts of creation, purgation, and destruction.

---

1 "The Dark Night" in Kavanaugh and Rodrigues, *Collected Works*, 416–17, 445.

2. Bergson cited in Guerlac, *Thinking in Time*, 74–75.

3. Walsh, *Bill Viola*, 52.

Figure 3.

Figure 4.

Figure 5.

The Passions

On a more unassuming scale (measuring only 19" x 15"), yet part of the larger *Passions* series, is Viola's *Man of Sorrows* (see Figure 6), which draws on a theme central to the history of Christian art, Christ as the Man of Sorrows, a name which derives from the Book of Isaiah in which a humble suffering servant is foreseen as the messiah, savior of the Jewish people.[4] Here is the Isaian text:

> He was despised and rejected by others;
> a man of suffering and acquainted with infirmity;
> and as one from whom others hide their faces
> he was despised, and we held him no account.
> Surely he has borne our infirmities
> And carried our diseases;
> Yet we accounted him stricken,
> Struck down by God, and afflicted (Isa 53:3–4).

4. The piece was recently featured in the 2011 exhibition, *Passion in Venice*, at the Museum of Biblical Art in New York, an exhibition comprised of more than sixty works of art, ranging from painting and sculpture to prints and illuminated manuscripts, all exploring the rich and multivalent theme of "passion" within the Venetian artistic tradition.

Figure 6.

Viola's *Man of Sorrows* is the portrait of an anonymous individual's encounter with deep sorrow and loss. Like traditional devotional icons of the suffering Christ, we are presented the image of an ordinary man in tears, weeping without explanation in a pain that only intensifies, and framed in standard portrait style displayed on a small, portable, table-top flat-panel screen. The artist describes the image as offering a painfully "privileged window into a private, intimate moment of extreme anguish." Throughout the slow-moving sequence (approximately eleven minutes), the man remains

> . . . immersed in a world of sorrow. Waves of emotion open and unfold subtly across the man's face, his actions . . . further slowed and expanded in time during playback. With the image cycle continuously repeating and his suffering unrelenting, he remains in a state of perpetual tears and eternal sadness.[5]

How, then, *do* we respond? With fear or trust? With disdain or hospitality? How *should* we respond? Do we engage or look away? We are caught here in moment of appeal to moral conscience, a sacred summons to the holiness in the everyday.

A closely related work, *Dolorosa* (see Figure 7), from 2000, similarly depicts and evokes suffering. Two images now, a woman and a man, presented

5. Walsh, *Bill Viola*, 104.

like family photographs on individual digital flat screens, framed together like a hinged votive image. Related but separate, the artist describes, the "two are seen in the throes of extreme sorrow, with tears streaming down their cheeks. Their actions unfold in slow motion and the sequence is presented on a continuously repeating loop, placing the individual's temporary state of crying within the larger domain of perpetual tears and eternal sorrow."[6] Speaking more broadly of Viola's work, art historian and curator Michael Rush writes: "Displayed as single projections, diptychs, or triptychs each of these works is characterized by extremely slowed down movements of men and women in modern dress portraying 'characters' from the earlier paintings. Eyelids can take several minutes to close, as do arms raising up in supplication or extending in an embrace."[7] In our examples here, Viola is clearly aware of the widespread and powerful spiritual practice of faithful meditation on the image of the suffering Christ and sorrowing Virgin, and has studied late medieval images of this kind, such as Dieric Bouts's *Christ as Salvator Mundi* (see Figure 8), (c.1450) and *Mater Dolorosa* (see Figure 9), c.1480/1500. In *Salvator Mundi* Christ is posed frontally with his attention locked on the viewer. Viola's denim-shirted man weeps; his head, first inclined to one side looks up in supplication, brow furrowed and tears stream down his cheeks; his pain deepens, peaks, then subsides. But he never shrinks from our view. Instead, like Christ as the Man of Sorrows, he holds himself up to be contemplated, urging an ethical response. Here again is Isaiah:

Figure 7.

6. Ibid., 76.
7. Rush, *Video Art*, 137.

Figure 8.

He was oppressed, and he was afflicted,
Yet he did not open his mouth;
Like a lamb that is led to the slaughter,
And like a sheep that before its shearers is silent,
So he did not open his mouth.
By a perversion of justice he was taken away.
Who could have imagined his future?
For he was cut off from the land of the living,
Stricken for the transgression of my people (Isa 53:7–8).

Much of the *Passions* series, and other even more recent work, is in fact indebted to Viola's studies in the 1990s of Western art, particularly Medieval and Renaissance devotional painting, and a return to the functions of such art as a path to spiritual growth. Far more than contemporary restagings of art history, however, Viola's deceptively spare video and sound installations go beyond representation to pursue the ancient theme of revelation within the layers of human consciousness, challenging a viewer's expectations and conditioned viewing patterns. Most were shot on 35-mm film at very high speed and slowed down drastically, so that almost imperceptible shifts are observed; these are then transferred to digital video and played on flat screens. Viola himself explains that these works are meant to "cultivat[e] knowledge of how to be in the world, for going through life. It is useful for developing a deeper understanding, in a very personal, subjective, private way, of your own experiences."[8] Critic Donald Kuspit accounts for this poetics of light and time as "conveying a radical state of consciousness inseparable from the awareness of mystical personal sensation. They seem not just to alter one's consciousness but to uproot one's being."[9]

Figure 9.

8. Walsh, *Bill Viola*, 75.
9. Kuspit, "Bill Viola," 145.

The Quintet Series

In one sub-group of *The Passions*, the so-called "Quintet" series—comprising *The Quintet of the Astonished* (see Figure 10) , *The Quintet of Remembrance* (see Figure 11), *The Quintet of the Silent* (see Figure 12) and *The Quintet of the Unseen* (see Figure 13)—the artist stages four groups of five figures in individual videos to explore universal human emotions of sorrow, anger, fear, joy, rapture—scenes much distilled from the narrative environments of earlier work like *Room for St. John of the Cross*. Each unifying theme—bewilderment, memory, the unspoken and the unseen—are familiar tropes by now. The series, we know, was inspired by the group of four figures surrounding the central figure of Christ in Hieronymus Bosch's painting of c.1490–1500, *Christ Mocked (The Crowning of Thorns)* at the National Gallery, London (see Figure 14); it depicts four soldiers, beholding the face of Christ in the center who does not return their mocking looks within the pictorial narrative but rather gazes directly out of it, *at us* the beholder. In Peter Sellers's evocative description of the Bosch painting as it is seen by Viola we should hold in mind Viola's *Man of Sorrows*:

Figure 10.

In the center, the face of God looks directly at us. The gaze is gentle . . . but increasingly penetrating as it makes an appeal to conscience. Christ's eyes look out of the painting, cross time and space, and meet our own. His eyes meet our eyes, and search our heart. Jesus makes us the witness. The choices are now ours. The responsibility is now ours. We can't pretend that we don't know or that we haven't noticed. The act of witness to suffering is life-changing. For some it will mean another hardening of the heart.

For others it is the birth of compassion. We are the observer, and now we are the participant.[10]

Figure 11.

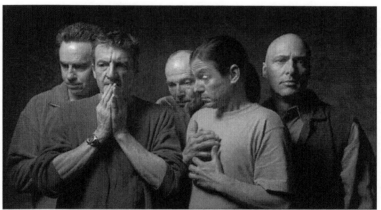

Figure 12.

This crossing of time and space in which occurs the meeting of gazes, the viewer's and Christ's, is what Emmanuel Levinas will call, as we shall shortly see, the "naked appeal of the Other," the "silent speaking" that demands ethical response. In a spatio-temporal sense, there is, in that moment of beholding, a circular turning back, a semantic exchange where subject and object, self and other, are one. This moment in which the boundaries between divine and human, self and other, dissolve is a moment of mystical union.

10. Walsh, *Bill Viola*, 172.

Figure 13.

In a journal entry describing the work he planned to make at the National Gallery's invitation, Viola noted:

> Quintet of the Astonished: odd but careful spatial grouping, horizontal aspect ratio, high-speed film, delicate lighting, wardrobe character types, Bosch's *Christ Mocked* in the National Gallery of London, the shifting surface of emotion and relation. Individuals run through a compressed range of conflicting emotions from laughing to crying, shot in high-speed film, displayed in high resolution, pristine, hyper-real. The emotions come and go so gradually, it is hard to tell where one begins and the other leaves off. Relations between the figures become fluid and shifting.[11]

In slow-motion replay that inhabits a space-time all its own, and resulting in exaggerated and high-definition gestures and expressions that change so gradually we observe nuances that would barely be noticed in real time, real space, or real life, Viola captures, as he puts it, "what the old masters didn't paint" (Bergson's "what is happening in the interval")—that is, the in-between of emotion that springs from beneath the visible surface of observable phenomena, at the edge of perception in a liminal space of pure possibility where sensations are heightened—a place of "visionary merger with the divine," as Donald Kuspit puts it.[12]

---

11. Ibid., 33.
12. Kuspit, "Deep TV," 89.

Figure 14.

In each of the four works that comprise the *Quintet* series, five people are positioned close together, as individually and collectively they experience "a wave of intense emotion that threatens to overwhelm them"[13] in a kind of psychic disintegration. As the sequence begins, their expressions change, at first nearly imperceptibly—but made visible through extreme slow motion—as the emotion, unique to each person surges to an acute level. After peaking, it subsides, leaving each person thoroughly depleted, physically and psychologically. In another quite telling notebook entry, here on the idea of self-emptying and the annihilation of the ego through suffering, the artist identifies the apophatic breakthrough of such liminal events:

> Breakdown—breakthrough. Reach the peak of physical exis-
> tence—It is no longer possible to be in the Body. The pressure
> is unbearable. The load unsustainable. The weight pulling on
> the fettered soul excruciating. Release comes as a violent explo-
> sion—All emotions condense at a single point, a unity, and then
> race outward, splintering into shards and fragments flying off in
> all directions. The aftermath of this harrowing journey through

13. Walsh, *Bill Viola*, 37

the narrowest of apertures is both a release from suffering and the manifestation of that suffering—Joy and Sorrow, Exhaustion and Strength. Breakdown and Breatkhrough.[14]

In the *Quintets*, while in close proximity throughout the experience, the five individuals undergo the mounting emotion, with minimal direct interaction with or even acknowledgement of each other, but at the same time together in an experience of communal suffering, shared but articulated across differences. The figures maintain that dissociation from one another we see among Christ's executioners in the Bosch painting, despite the tightly enclosed area. Likewise, the group stands before an empty background with no narrative setting or reference to the outside world.[15] In preparing his actors for the *Quintet* video shoots, Viola provided each of them copies of poems from books in his own library by St. John of the Cross: "I wanted to give them historical reference points," he said, "people who had been there before, in the regions of the human self that I wanted them to address."[16]

Five Angels for the Millennium (2001)

Another multi-part work, again a sub-group within the *Passions* project, is *Five Angels for the Millennium*, 2001, which consists of five 7 x 10-foot individual video sequences each showing a clothed man emerging out of or disappearing into a pool of water—taken collectively, an immersive and engulfing experience of sound and light. In *Departing Angel* (see Figure 15) a single figure floats gradually into view and up to the surface accompanied by faint sound; in *Birth Angel* (see Figure 16), the figure shoots more dramatically through the frame as the ambient sound mounts; in *Fire Angel* (see Figure 17) the figure is completely submerged in water that has now taken on the color of a deep blood-red, while in *Ascending Angel* (see Figure 18) he is seen floating more tranquilly, face down, then rising, and *Creation Angel* (see Figure 19), where, amidst a crescendo of sound he appears from the back with arms outstretched in a cruciform gesture. Playing simultaneously and continuously repeating, the images are projected directly onto the walls of a large

14. Ibid., 166.

15. Similar images in both composition and theme that Viola studied and drew upon during his time at the Getty, include: Andrea Mantegna's *Adoration of the Magi*, c. 1500 and Dieric Bouts's, *The Annunciation*, c. 1450–55.

16. Walsh, *Bill Viola*, 35. Included in Viola's personal library he brought with him to the Getty were also the works of Meister Eckhart and the seminal study *The Art of Devotion in the Late Middle Ages, 1300–1500* by Henk Van Os (1995), and studies by scholar Victor Stoichita on the visionary experiences of Spanish Baroque artists.

dark room, resonating with Burkean emphasis on the sublimity in darkness and obscurity. As Getty Director Emeritus John Walsh describes in the *Passions* exhibition catalogue:

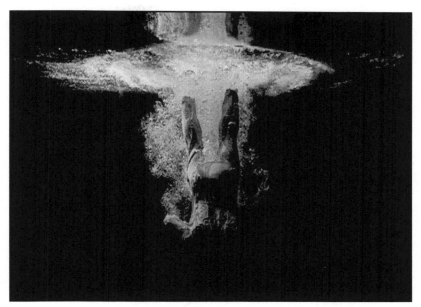

Figure 15.

Figure 16.

Figure 17.

Figure 18.

Figure 19.

The "angel" in each appears infrequently on each screen, breaking through the surface in a sudden explosion of light and sound
that interrupts an otherwise peaceful watery landscape. Weightless and motionless, the human figure enters into the depths of
a mysterious underwater world, a luminous void of unknown
dimensions, where the laws of physics seem suspended and the
borders between the infinite cosmos and the finite human body
merge.[17]

Long attracted to the reflective, transformative and symbolic properties of water, the artist explores the ways in which water sustains, cleanses,
blesses, and takes life away. Birth and death, each conceived as a dramatic
transition in consciousness rather than as a conclusive beginning or a defin-
itive end, are given shape as unfathomable mysteries. In an interview with
Viola, art historian Hans Belting refers to these apparitions as "an act performed in front of the beholder." "In the context of religion," Belting elaborates, "the most important images were those that appeared to the very few
and granted them privilege. An image appearing is an image happening."[18]

17. Walsh, *Bill Viola*, 146.
18. Ibid., 216.

The video sequences, the original length of which ran only thirty-five to forty seconds, are slow and meditative, and take considerable time (ten to fifteen minutes) and patience to absorb, wherein the viewer is engulfed in sensory experience—random and unsynchronized accelerations and decelerations—within a darkened room. Viola explains: "There are no cuts in the sequences, no montage in the traditional sense. There is only a gradual permutation in the continuous, inexorable progression toward or away from the moment of the plunge into the water . . . This 'deep seeing' is a vital part of human experience that draws on our powers of inner concentration and identification, both characteristic of the visionary experience."[19] Philosopher Cynthia Freeland, in language marshaled to conjure a sense of the Kantian (mathematic and dynamic) sublime, further interprets the work:

> Each of the gigantic panels dwarfs us, but they are also dispersed, so that one cannot view them together. We cannot take in what we are seeing or hearing. We cannot make sense of what is showing on any one screen, nor understand how the five figures are related. The low roars and bubbling sounds seem to speak an alien tongue . . . The sensory overload presents an intellectual conundrum. Despite this, we may feel exalted because the pieces are so stimulating. They are exhilarating because of their carefully coordinated scale, vividness, their sheer bursts of energy. At certain points when we dimly grasp that a body is emerging . . . from the water, the works suggest the enormity of our own creative powers.[20]

In our following the illusion (it isn't quite a narrative) of the images—or attempting to—Viola urges us to contemplate how the limits of the image and its manipulations of space and time—velocity, simultaneity, succession—force us to reevaluate what we have really seen, our perception of reality; we are left positioned on the boundary between the visible and the invisible, or more accurately, we are left with the invisibility of the once seen (the angel) and the anticipation and knowledge of its return.[21] Amidst a swelling and ebbing soundtrack—heard before anything is seen, what Rhys Davies calls "the sound of being"[22]—and unsynchronized percussions of figures striking the water's surface and plunging beneath it, Viola creates, as the artist himself has tellingly called it "an enveloping emotional experience like that of a church."[23]

19. Ibid., 217.
20. Freeland in Townsend, *Art of Bill Viola*, 38.
21. See Kuspit, "Bill Viola: Deconstructing Presence," in London, *Bill Viola*, 73–80.
22. Davies in Townsend, *Art of Bill Viola*, 152.
23. Ibid., 48.

In fact, *Five Angels*, as a multi-part work, is perhaps most reminiscent of Viola's earlier (1996) single projection installation, *The Messenger* (see Figure 20), commissioned by and installed at Durham Cathedral to mark the UK Year of the Visual Arts. That controversial piece—controversial as it was originally intended to be projected onto the great west wall of the Cathedral and seen down the length of the nave from the altar, but then prudishly screened from general view—begins similarly in portentous darkness; then, slowly, an emergent light takes shape, and the form of a naked man gradually rises from the depths of water until he breaks the surface with a climactic gasp of breath as his eyes open, only to descend and disappear back into the dark depths until the cycle begins again. David Jasper has accounted for the work's multivalent theological references:

> Many people seemed to want to see *The Messenger* in purely Christian terms. Viewed through the [baptismal] font, it was interpreted as an image of the mystery of Initiation, of the baptismal immersion with Christ and the rising with him into new life . . . But the complex, universal symbolism of water was appropriated by Christianity as it drew upon a rich heritage of biblical stories—from the myths of creation to Noah's flood, the Exodus through the Red Sea, the crossing of Jordan into the promised land of Canaan, and the baptism of Jesus by John.[24]

And while indeed thoroughly infused with Christian symbol, Viola's own statements and writings indicate a wider set of resonant spiritualities captured in this piece and in his work in general. For instance, in an interview in 1997 with poet and cultural critic Lewis Hyde, Viola was asked specifically about the connections in his work to spiritual life. After acknowledging his Christian (Episcopalian) upbringing and his later encounters with Eastern religions, the artist remarked:

> I guess the connection ultimately, if I can say it in one encapsulated way, has to do with an acknowledgement or awareness or recognition that there is something above, beyond, below, beneath what's in front of our eyes, what our daily life is focused on. There's another dimension that you just know is there, that can be a source of real knowledge, and the quest for connecting with that and identifying that is the whole impetus for me to cultivate these experiences and to make my work. And, on a larger scale, it is also the driving force behind all religious endeavors. There is an unseen world out there and we are living in it.[25]

24. David Jasper in Townsend, *Art of Bill Viola*, 184.
25. Ross, *Bill Viola*, 143.

Figure 20.

Also shown at Durham Cathedral at the same time was *The Crossing* (1996) discussed above. "These works embody," Hans Belting summarized in the interview with the artist cited above, an "epiphanic character . . . In them, you always feel the presence of a threshold which the figures have to confront and cross . . . Thus, such appearances relate metaphorically to birth and death, but if I see it correctly, they more accurately reference a spiritual birth and death within the individual."[26] Once again, Viola presents the viewer of his work with that sense of *liminality* and its inherent vulnerability:

26. Walsh, *Bill Viola*, 216.

To the European mind the reverberant characteristics of the interior of the Gothic cathedral are inextricably linked with a deep sense of the sacred and tend to evoke strong associations with both the internal private space of contemplation and the larger realm of the ineffable . . . Cathedrals . . . embody concepts derived from the rediscovery of the works of the ancient Greeks, particularly those of Plato and Pythagoras, and their theories of the correspondence between the macrocosm and the microcosm, expression in the language of sacred number, proportion, and harmony, and that manifest themselves in the science of sound and music. These design concepts were not considered to be the work of man, or merely functions of architectural practice, but represented the divine underlying principles of the universe itself.[27]

Jean-Luc Marion and the Saturated Phenomenon

In reckoning with the idea of representing the invisible, Bill Viola's art may be situated within postmodern notions of the "unrepresentable." Theologically this invokes the idea of seeing God in "glimpses" or "traces," never knowing God completely, but only in part—or as St. Paul had it "in a mirror dimly" (1 Corinthians 13:12). Moreover, the apophatic description of God as an abstract experience, not conceptually definable in terms of space and location, nor confinable to conventions of time—God as transcendent of essence—can be theorized within the context of "unknowability" and, as I want to show, French phenomenologist and mystical theologian Jean-Luc Marion's "God without Being." While Marion's philosophy is complex, central to his argument about a God free of all categories of Being—and therefore its particular relevance to this study—is his distinction between what he characterizes as the *idol* and the *icon*, "two modes of apprehension of the divine invisibility."[28]

Marion's theory of the *icon* is a theory of the way the invisible (unseen) reveals itself, and as such the icon is defined in opposition to the idol. A thing or being becomes an *idol* when the human gaze directed toward it allows itself to be completed or satisfied by this visible thing or being. Thus the "idol" is essentially a confirming concept of God. The intention of the human gaze is completely absorbed in the sight/site of the idol. This means that intention and gaze allow themselves to be fixed on a given visible shape.

27. Viola, *Reasons for Knocking*, 154–55.
28. Marion, *God Without Being*, 9.

As Victor Kal has argued, intention and gaze do not *see through* the visible; rather, they are enraptured *with* the visible.[29] The idol, then, is the representation of God adjusted to human, finite standards; it is the human agent who is in control of the viewing, who is in possession of the viewed.

A helpful analogy—in the specific context of Viola it serves as more than analogy here—may be with the Renaissance construct of *linear* or *scientific perspective*, a mathematical and technical procedure for measuring and controlling a three-dimensional view onto a two-dimension plane, giving the effect of distance—what we've come to mean as "having a perspective" on something, or putting information "into perspective." Simply put, perspective (in painting) is a visual system by which an illusion of depth is created by geometric means on a flat surface, and organized from a single point of view. In perspective construction, the viewer, rather than the world seen, has priority. The appearance of things in pictorial space is a function of their distance from the viewer. The picture is, then, the artist's (and ultimately viewer's) construct; it is his ordering of a view that posits a unity perceived at a distance from the viewer. And the perception of that unity and mastery over it is contingent upon setting up the distance.

Viola himself confirms the appropriateness of this analogy in referring to Renaissance picture construction as "new technical systems of art based on optics and sight [which] were supplanting medieval schemes based on modes of an invisible, spiritual reality."[30] Vision, in this sense, is not a matter of multiple, simultaneous, and perhaps conflicting observations, experiences and impulses, as it was in pre-modern depiction; rather, it is a hierarchically constructed relationship to the known world; the world as fitted to our measure and position, where we have a clear, confirming, and reassuring sense of our place and proportion relative to the "vision."[31] It presupposes that the beholder's eye occupies a fixed point in space; thus a perspectively organized picture situates the viewer in place in order to see the view "correctly"—it is a rationalization of seeing.

Similarly, Marion's idol is the *human* experience of the divine; it refers to the structure of thought on God within human limits, God as manifest

---

29. Bulhof and ten Kate, *Flight of the Gods*, 157.

30. Walsh, *Bill Viola*, 219.

31. This Western concept of the picture as seen through a window contrasts significantly with that in the East, as art historian Ananda Coomaraswamy showed and whose writing Viola studied; in the latter, a different model of seeing "neither freezes the images in a moment of time nor fixes it 'out there' as an object, but reflects it back into the space of the viewer's mind." This observation is made by, and cited from, David Jasper in his essay on Viola's *Messenger*, in Townsend, *Art of Bill Viola*, 189.

presence, grounded in knowledge.[32] "The idol," the philosopher argues in *God Without Being*, "consigns the divine to the measure of a human gaze,"[33] which St. John of the Cross had called "vanity" and "doll-dressing," "nothing more than idols upon which they [the vainly pious] center their joy."[34] As a result, the gaze creates the idol, and the onlooker is fully satisfied by what he sees. Marion calls this way of seeing "idolatry." The idol is created by the desire to see and fix what is seen; the idol is exactly there where the gaze stops, and as such the idol is like a mirror; it merely reflects my desires—it does not allow a "beyond." That which is reflected in the mirror is the gaze itself, the gaze obsessed *by* itself. I see nothing but my own gaze, my own intention. There is no Other there, it is all Me. Viola echoes this idea when, in conversation with Hans Belting who had made reference to the story of Narcissus's reflection and self-love, responds: "That's wonderful—an image that is evoked or created by the observer to fulfill a desire or function . . . a creative image, but a hazardous one."[35] The idol may be a "picture" of God, but cut to the size and limits of the human imagination. Philosophically, the idol takes the shape of an idea or concept—and conceptualization means assimilation by human imagination.[36]

The *icon*, by contrast, represents a non-conceptual, non-idolized "appearance" of God. The icon is not produced by the human gaze; rather, "the icon summons a gaze."[37] It is this *summoning* I wish to highlight here. The theology of the icon, Marion observes, is found in Colossians 1:15: "He is the *eikon* of the invisible God . . .," incomprehensible by nature and therefore inaccessible to human intentionality. And that "He"—Christ, for St. Paul, the visible *eikon* of God—may well be, for us, the invisible God in the visible Other. The *icon*, then, overcomes the mirror and the intentional gaze, and itself claims or summons the gaze of the onlooker. In other words, the visible icon, qua object, refers *beyond itself* to the invisible. "The icon does not make the invisible *tangibly* present. The icon makes the invisible *as invisible* present for the glance. The icon can be seen and refers beyond itself."[38] Marion summarizes this in *God Without Being*: "In the idol, the gaze of man is frozen in its mirror; in the icon, the gaze of man is lost in *the invisible gaze that visibly engages him*" (my emphasis). The icon "unbalances human

---

32. Marion, *Idol and Distance*.

33. Marion, *God Without Being*, 10.

34. Kavanaugh and Rodrigues, *Completed Works*, 332.

35. Walsh, *Bill Viola*, 207.

36. See in this context Jonkers and Welten, *God in France*, 190–91.

37. Ibid., 158.

38. Ibid.

sight in order to engulf it in infinite depth;" it is about the "presence of a non-object."[39] I do not focus upon the icon, my gaze does not rest or settle on it; rather the *icon focuses on me*. The icon is the intentional gaze of the *other* in me; Marion refers to it as the "perfect reversal" of intentionality. The icon approaches me, it *gives* itself.[40] It is a soliciting force. We might think back, for instance, on the call for our response in Viola's *Man of Sorrows*, and, as with the medieval icon, in the crossing of time and space within the encounter between Self and Other, self and divine stranger, is Levinas's "naked appeal of the Other." "The stranger before me," writes theologian Richard Kearney, "both *is* God (as transcendent Guest) and *is not* God (as screen of my projections and presumptions)." Kearny elaborates:

> Out of this tension faith leaps. There can be no immediate ap-
> propriation of the divine Other as my "own," but only a relation-
> ship to someone other than myself who is, so to speak, *like* me
> while remaining irreducibly *unlike* me qua Other.[41]

Observance (2002)

This is precisely what I think is occurring in Viola's *Quintets* and, more directly perhaps in his *Observance* (see Figures 21 and 22) from 2002 which
substitutes the traditional notion of a painting as window through which
the viewer looks at the image of the world, for the religious icon which calls
the viewer into the divine image. Viola, again, resists the traditional definition of the picture:

> The idea of art as a kind of diagram has for the most part not
> made it down from the Middle Ages into modern European
> consciousness. The Renaissance was the turning point, and the
> subsequent history of Western art, can be viewed as the progres-
> sive distancing of the arts away from the sacred and towards
> the profane . . . Painting became an architectural, spatial form,
> which the viewer experienced by physically walking through it
> . . . What Brunelleschi [the inventor of perspective] achieved was
> the personification of the image, the creation of a "point of view"
> and its identification with a place in real space. In doing so, he
> elevated the position of the individual viewer to an integral part of
> the picture by encoding this presence . . . The picture became an

39. Marion, *Crossing of the Visible*, 60–61.
40. Jonkers and Welten, *God in France*, 192–93.
41. Kearney, *Anatheism*, 15.

opaque mirror for the viewer, and the viewer, in turn, became the embodiment of the painter, "completing the picture" . . .[42]

In *Observance* a queue of people—different ages, races, ethnicities—moves forward slowly, steadily, solemnly and ritualistically toward the viewer. Singly, one after the other, each pauses at the head of the line, visibly weakened by private yet shared emotion, their gazes trained on some unknown object or unseen (by us) tragedy. In prompting his actors Viola urged them to come forward to look at "something they'd rather not see . . . to say goodbye to someone who'd left them."[43] In sorrow or despair or grief they are witness to some tragedy or loss, like a modern-day lamentation—just out of sight beyond the frame, mesmerized by some petitioning force operating within our space. Sometimes gently touching, overlapping, or occasionally exchanging glances between them as they pass, they are unified by their shared desire to reach the front and engage with whatever or whomever is there, effecting a "crossing of gazes" as Marion would have it, two currents of consciousness pressing upon each other. There is a private intimacy in their silence, yet they urge us somehow to participate in their emotions.

Figure 21.   Figure 22.

42. Viola, *Reasons for Knocking*, 103, 105, 198–202.
43. Walsh, *Bill Viola*, 53.

Levinas calls this the "address," the proffering to and petitioning force of the other, seeing in the other the inescapable ethical appeal that obligates me. He refers to this as the Face of the Other that speaks—makes meaning—not in a language of words or sounds, but as a call, a beckoning, a "Saying" (*Dire*) of our responsibility in relation to the Other. In this crossing of awarenesses we recognize the other person facing us as a free and self-determining subject with an ethical claim upon me rather than as an object at my disposal. The Face of the Other *is* the wordless discourse, the silent and unconditional ethical appeal that manifests pre-ontological intelligibility before language; Levinas's is a philosophy deeply indebted to the apophatic and mystical tradition. Here William Franke glosses the philosopher:

> For Levinas, the face-to-face relation of one human being with another is an origin for the intelligibility of things that does not presuppose any prior disclosedness of beings. Our being in relation to others, blindly and helplessly, without any conscious control or conceptual mastery, precedes all sense and intelligibility of objects that we are able to grasp and conceptualize . . . The ineffable transcendence discovered in the ethical relation to the Other cannot be comprehended and articulated, but rather dis-articulates me from my origin as self-conscious subject and freely choosing agent.[44]

What occurs in Bill Viola's *Observance* is the viewer's/my receptiveness to the world that, coming from the "other," resounds in him/me. We are open to being "caught upon" by the image, instead of having authority of visual (and intellectual) possession over it; we are called into an aesthetic and ethical posture of *attentiveness*. Richard Kearny has referred to this as a moment of "holy insecurity," an experience of "dispossessive bewilderment" wherein we become "attuned to the acoustics of the Other."[45] Like Marion's icon, these images preserve transcendence by refusing the mirroring function of the idol, such that the viewer finds himself *envisaged* by the other. This is not unlike the "crossings" of ordinary space and time and the elements of "incarnational space" that occurs in the performance of sacramental ritual; and this itself has echoes in St. John of the Cross's descriptions of ecstatic absorption in God and his own near loss of consciousness of his immediate surroundings, an experience nourished by the sacraments and liturgy. It is liturgical worship that activates all the senses, such that our bodies fully participate in the divine. And as Viola accounts for *Five Angels* and his other large-scale installations like *Observance* and

44. Franke, *On What Cannot Be Said*, 27–29.
45. Kearney, *Anatheism*, 8.

the *Quintets*, these works "speak[s] to us in the language of the body . . . This corporeal language is essential in order to speak of certain things that can't be discussed in any other way; or, to put it differently: these subjects need to be transmitted through bodily experience, otherwise they would only be descriptions."[46]

These "subjects," or "selves-in-process" as I've referred to them, are subjects-in-community, and thus profoundly ethical—in *Observance* the figures mourn loss in a communal setting. One is drawn *toward* the sublime and *away from* false and distorting constructions of the self, experienced perhaps in terms of astonishment because unaccustomed to such encounters; it is a profound relationship that provides the occasion for what theologian Stanley Hauerwas has called "unselfings"[47]—a disciplined overcoming of the self. "Self-annihilation" (the undoing of egoistic self), we recall Viola as saying, "becomes a necessary means to transcendence and liberation."[48]

46. Ibid., 219.

47. See Bychkov and Fodor, *Theological Aesthetics After Von Balthasar*, 192.

48. Walsh, *Bill Viola*, 52.

5

The Secret Tongue of the Heart
Some Final Remarks

SO HOW, IN THE end, *does* one speak of God, a god who is not the result of theoretical constructions or psychological desires? How do we acknowledge and find meaning in the summoning soliciting gaze of the Other? Doesn't the apophatic gesture set up too much distance, too radical a separation between us and the divine? "Negative theology," as Jacques Derrida has claimed, "means (to say) very little, almost nothing, perhaps something other than something. Whence its inexhaustible exhaustion. . ."[1] For Derrida, in *Sauf le Nom* (1993), the question, much like for our apophatics, is how we may save the divine "name" by refusing to articulate its content; his answer, however, is a kind of mystical atheism. Moreover, as Chris Boesel and Catherine Keller argue with respect to apophatic mysticism, "This transcendence smacks of indifference (and so, ethically, of quietism) in the face of the needs, desires, and unjust sufferings of an embodied life."[2]

We can, I think, circle back to Kant one last time to consider the conjoining of ethics and aesthetics toward what I've called an ethical sublime, a sublime now not in relation to nature but in relation to others and to oneself. Compellingly, Kant had argued in his earlier treatise *Observations on the Feeling of the Beautiful and the Sublime*:

---

1. Derrida, *Sauf le nom*, in Franke, *On What Cannot Be Said*, 453.
2. Boesel and Keller, *Apophatic Bodies*, 3.

But what if the secret tongue of the heart speaks in this manner: "I must come to the aid of that man, for he suffers; not that he were perhaps my friend or companion, nor that I hold him amenable to repaying the good deed with gratitude later on. There is now no time to reason and delay with questions; he is a man, and whatever befalls men, that also concerns me." Then his conduct sustains itself on the highest ground of benevolence in human nature, and is extremely sublime, because of its unchangeability as well as of the universality of its application.[3]

Marion's *God Without Being*, we said, was an attempt to think God without or beyond the language of being or ontology. "Traditional metaphysical language," Christina Gschwandtner argues, "that has been used to speak of God is inadequate to such a task."[4] It is this critique of onto-theology that perhaps links Marion most closely to his former teacher Derrida (and the idea of presence *sous rature*), and to the failure of classical metaphysics generally. For Marion, such efforts to designate God philosophically as ultimate being not only fail by their inadequacy in speaking of a divine, but can even be considered idolatrous.[5] God cannot be an object of human knowledge, subordinate to the epistemological demands of a knower. Such a knowing ego which grounds all reality within a "metaphysics of presence" involves the notion that the world can be divided into such subject-object relations; it posits a world made up of objects the attributes of which, and therefore names and descriptions, can be predicated. Hence, Marion's language of incomprehensibility, blinding light, *saturation* and *excess*, which diverges from Derrida and his deconstructionist acolytes as fullness does from emptiness.

Central to Marion's phenomenology is the concept of the *saturated phenomenon*, the spilling over of all bounds of content which conveys something of God, and it is that surplus which can be tied directly to our extended reading of the Kantian "sublime." Marion's saturated phenomenon is, as John Caputo has glossed it, "the idea that there are phenomena of such overwhelming givenness or overflowing fulfillment that the intentional acts [such as conscious efforts at conceptualization . . .] aimed at these phenomena are overrun, flooded—or saturated."[6] Marion, then, can be situated within our earlier discussion of the (im)possibility of "naming" God—not, as the postmoderns would have it, in the sense

---

3. Quoted in Costelloe, *Sublime*, 205.

4. Gschwandtner, *Reading Jean-Luc Marion*, 3.

5. Ibid.

6. Caputo, Review of *The Erotic Phenomenon*, 164.

of the inexhaustible self-depletion of language, but rather in the sense of apophaticism's "excess of meaning."

Marion posits a phenomenality that is "saturated" or fulfilled—abundant phenomenon. This means it does not depend on my orientation or my intentionality or my interpretation. It blinds me, overriding my intentionality. Marion characterized it as an *excess*: again, I am blinded; there is too much light. On a similar note, "the spiritual light," wrote St. John of the Cross, "is so bright and so transcendent that it blinds . . ."[7] And this of course has roots in that most Platonic of images, the "dazzling darkness" experienced by the released prisoner in the Allegory of the Cave, as there his ascent toward the excess of brilliant light is so jarring as to cause pain and darkness—the price of contemplation of the "light" of truth. Darkness here is the excess of light, rather than its absence; Gregory of Nyssa called it "luminous darkness." And St. Paul asserts, in 1 Timothy 6:16, that God "dwells in unapproachable light."

Metaphysics for Marion is itself idolatrous precisely because it circumscribes the divine by a concept, a concept that supposes it can define—and thereby limit—God. And the notion of excess or saturation is not unlike the initial disappointment the mind experiences in the Kantian sublime wherein one is confronted with the limits of finite consciousness. In an interview with Richard Kearney, author of *The God Who May Be*, Marion speaks of this sense of disappointment:

> The very experience of the excess of intuition over significa-
> tion makes clear that the excess may be felt and expressed as
> disappointment. The experience of disappointment means that
> I marked an experience which I cannot understand, because I
> have no concept of it. So the excess and the disappointment can
> come together.[8]

This "disappointment" is the situation of encountering something without having the possibility to understand it. We must come to realize that it is an invitation not to comprehension, but to *participation*.

But, still, is God/the Divine Other too transcendent, without possibility for relationship? This is the question or critique Richard Kearney puts to Marion. Kearney argues instead for a *revelation* of God that doesn't speculate about Being or ontology but rather remarks on the experience of plenitude, and therefore the idea of a God of possibility and promise—a more hopeful notion than that which he imputes to Marion as "a divinity so far beyond-being that no heurmeneutics of interpreting, imagining, symbolizing, or

---

7. Kavanaugh and Rodrigues, *Complete Works*, 434.
8. Quoted in Gschwandtner, *Reading Jean-Luc Marion*, 78.

narrativizing is really acceptable," and where "God's alterity appears so utterly unnameable and apophatic that any attempt to throw heurmeneutic drawbridges between it and our finite means of language is deemed a form of idolatry."[9] Such negative, apophatic theology, Kearney claims, denies any possibility of narrative imagination, such that "the divine remains utterly unthinkable, unnamable, unrepresentable—that is, unmediatable."

While this notion of the abjectness (and preclusion) of God may very well be present in Derrida and postmodernist reveling in the bankruptcy of language as representation, Marion, I think, may be closer to our mystics in arguing not simply about this inadequacy but, despite it, urging us—as flawed human beings—to imagine nevertheless, to trust in a revelation and to be open to overwhelming promise of grace. (Even Derrida at one point allows in his 1993 *Memoirs of the Blind*, "I don't know, one has to believe."[10]) And indeed, St. John of the Cross, having experienced the grace of God, feels its loss that much more intensely. His is a suffering in love that is so much more than psychic anguish in the face of mere absence. A God real enough to be absent is real enough to be present.

Kearney's critique, however, is helpful for our purposes in articulating what is going on in Bill Viola's construction of just such an aesthetic—and theological—posture of openness and *attentiveness*. Kearney insists on a need for what he calls a "narrative heurmeneutics," according to which "religious language"—and I count Viola's efforts as such—"endeavor to say something . . . about the unsayable."[11] The art of Bill Viola, I have contended, opens our eyes to a new way for things one would not otherwise see, and a reaching for the uncontainable and for an inner life that resists the external necessities of existence—in other words, a theology (and technology) of *revelation*. It invites us to have the courage to welcome the unprecedented. Marion's phenomenology of possibility offers, I think, just such an aesthetics of *hope*. Kearny calls it a "creative not knowing," a "break with ingrained habits of thought and an open[ing] up [of] novel possibilities of meaning." "Without the abandonment of accredited certainties," he writes, "we remain inattentive to the advent of the strange; we ignore those moments of sacred enfleshment when the future erupts through the continuum of time."[12]

The meaning that Viola's art can portend may indeed be "present" as "absent." Its dialectic—of disclosure and concealment, presence and absence, or meaning as the promise of presence through embodied absence,

9. Ibid., 98.

10. Quoted in Townsend, *Art of Bill Viola*, 195.

11. Ibid.

12. Kearney, *Anatheism*, 7.

neither fully here and now nor entirely elsewhere and beyond—is what, I believe, makes his art replete with prophetic connotations of wonder, promise and futurity, as well as so engaging and so essential.

Bibliography

Addison, Joseph. *Collected Works, III.* Edited by H. Bohn. London, 1890.

Augustine. *On Christian Doctrine.* Oxford: Oxford University Press, 2008.

Belting, Hans. *Art History after Modernism.* Chicago: University of Chicago Press, 2003.

Bergson, Henri. *Creative Evolution.* Unabridged ed. Mineola, NY: Dover, 1998.

———. *Essai sur les donnés immédiates de la conscience.* Paris, 1924.

———. *An Introduction to Metaphysics.* New York, 1912.

Berry, Philippa, and Andrew Wernick, eds. *Shadow of Spirit: Postmodernism and Religion.* New York: Routledge 1993.

Boesel, Chris, and Catherine Keller, eds. *Apophatic Bodies: Negative Theology, Incarnation, and Relationality.* New York: Fordham University Press, 2010.

Bulhof, Ilse N., and Laurens ten Kate, eds. *Flight of the Gods: Philosophical Perspectives on Negative Theology.* New York: Fordham University Press, 2000.

Burke, Edmund. *A Philosophical Inquiry into the Origin of Our Ideas of the Sublime and the Beautiful.* Oxford World's Classics. Oxford: Oxford University Press, 2008.

Burwick, Frederick, and Paul Douglass. *The Crisis in Modernism: Bergson and the Vitalist Controversy.* Cambridge: Cambridge University Press, 1992.

Bychkov, Oleg V., and James Fodor, eds. *Theological Aesthetics after Von Balthasar.* Aldershot, UK: Ashgate, 2008.

Campbell, C. "Bill Viola: The Domain of the Human Condition." *Flash Art* 36/229 (March-April 2003) 88–91.

Caputo, John. Review of *The Erotic Phenomenon,* by Jean-Luc Marion. *Ethics* 118/1 (2007) 164–68.

Colledge, Edmund, and Bernard McGinn, trans. *Meister Eckhart: The Essential Sermons, Commentaries, Treatises, and Defense.* Mahwah, NJ: Paulist, 1981.

Cooley, Larry. "The Way to Ultimate Meaning in the Mystical Theology of St. John of the Cross." *Ultimate Reality and Meaning* 23/3 (2005) 201–27.

Costelloe, Timothy M., ed. *The Sublime: From Antiquity to the Present.* Cambridge: Cambridge University Pess, 2012.

Crowther, Paul. *The Kantian Sublime: From Morality to Art.* Oxford: Clarendon, 1989.

Danto, Arthur C. *The Abuse of Beauty: Aesthetics and the Concept of Art.* Chicago: Open Court, 2004.

Davies, Oliver, and Denys Turner, eds. *Silence and the Word: Negative Theology and Incarnation.* Cambridge: Cambridge University Press, 2002.

Deleuze, Gilles. *Bergsonism.* Translated by Hugh Tomlinson. New York: Zone, 1990.

Duve, Thierry de. *Look: 100 Years of Contemporary Art.* Amsterdam: Ludion, 2001.

Eco, Umberto. *Art and Beauty in the Middle Ages.* New Haven, CT: Yale University Press, 1985.

Elkins, James. *On the Strange Place of Religion in Contemporary Art.* New York: Routledge, 2004.

———. *Pictures and Tears: A History of People Who Have Cried in Front of Paintings.* New York: Routledge, 2001.

Elkins, James, and David Morgan, eds. *Re-Enchantment.* New York: Routledge, 2009.

Foster, Hal, ed. *Postmodern Culture.* London: Pluto, 1993.

Franke, William, ed. *On What Cannot Be Said: Apophatic Discourses in Philosophy, Religion, Literature, and the Arts.* 2 vols. Notre Dame: University of Notre Dame Press, 2007.

Gablik, Suzi. *The Reenchantment of Art.* New York: Thames & Hudson, 1991.

Garcia-Rivera, Alejandro. "On a New List of Aesthetic Categories." In *Theological Aesthetics after Von Balthasar*, edited by Olga V. Bychkov and James Fodor, 169–85. Aldershot, UK: Ashgate, 2008.

Griffin, Emilie, ed. *The Cloud of Unknowing.* New York: HarperOne, 2004.

Gschwandtner, Christina. *Reading Jean-Luc Marion: Exceeding Metaphysics.* Bloomington: Indiana University Press, 2007.

Guerlac, Suzanne. *Thinking in Time: An Introduction to Henri Bergson.* Ithaca, NY: Cornell University Press, 2006.

Heartney, Eleanor. *Postmodern Heretics: Catholic Imagination in Contemporary Art.* New York: Midmarch Arts, 2004.

Hedges, Chris. *Empire of Illusion: The End of Literacy and the Triumph of Spectacle.* New York: Nation, 2009.

Hoffmann, Roald, and Iain Boyd Whyte, eds. *Beyond the Finite: The Sublime in Art and Science.* Oxford: Oxford University Press, 2011.

Jonkers, Peter, and Rudd Welten, eds. *God in France: Eight Contemporary French Thinkers on God.* Leuven: Peeters, 2005.

Kant, Immanuel. *The Critique of Judgement.* Translated by James Creed Meredith. Oxford: Oxford University Press, 1952.

Kavanaugh, Kieran, and Otilio Rodrigues, trans. *The Collected Works of Saint John of the Cross.* Washington, DC: ICS, 1991.

Kearney, Richard. *Anatheism: Returning to God After God.* New York: Columbia University Press, 2010.

Kristeva, Julia. *The Kristeva Reader.* Edited by Toril Moi. New York: Columbia University Press, 1986.

———. *Revolution in Poetic Language.* New York: Columbia University Press, 1984.

Kuspit, Donald. "Bill Viola: The Passing." *Artforum* 32 (September 1993) n.p.

———. "Deep TV: Bill Viola's Via Negativa." *Artforum* 33 (May 1995) n.p.

Lefebvre, Alexandre, and Melanie White, eds. *Bergson, Politics, and Religion.* Durham, NC: Duke University Press, 2012.

London, Barbara, ed. *Bill Viola.* New York: Museum of Modern Art, 1987.

Lopez-Remiro, Miguel, ed. *Writings on Art: Mark Rothko.* New Haven, CT: Yale University Press, 2006.

Luibheid, Colm, trans. *Pseudo-Dionysius: The Complete Works.* Mahwah, NJ: Paulist, 1987.

Lyotard, Jean-Francois. *The Postmodern Explained: Correspondence 1982–1985*. Edited by Julian Pefanis and Morgan Thomas. Translated by Don Barry et al. Minneapolis: University of Minnesota Press, 1992.

———. "Presenting the Unpresentable: The Sublime." *Artforum* 20 (April 1992) 64–69.

Marion, Jean-Luc. *The Crossing of the Visible*. Translated by James K. A. Smith. Stanford: Stanford University Press, 2004.

———. *God Without Being*. Translated by T. Carlson. Chicago: University of Chicago Press, 1991.

———. *The Idol and Distance: Five Studies*. Translated by T. Carlson. New York: Fordham University Press, 2001.

———. *In the Self's Place: The Approach of Saint Augustine*. Translated by Jeffrey L. Kosky. Stanford: Stanford University Press, 2012.

Norris, Christopher. *Deconstruction: Theory and Practice*. London: Routledge, 1982.

O'Donnell, James. *Augustine*. Boston: Twayne, 1985.

Os, Henk van. *The Art of Devotion in the Late Middle Ages, 1300–1500*. Princeton, NJ: Princeton University Press, 1995.

Otto, Rudolf. *The Idea of the Holy*. Translated by John W. Harvey. New York: Oxford University Press, 1950.

Pokorn, Nike Kocijancic. "The Language and Discourse of *The Cloud of Unknowing*." *Literature and Theology* 11/4 (1997) 408–21.

Promey, Sally M. "The 'Return' of Religion in the Scholarship of American Art." *The Art Bulletin* 85 (September 2003) 581–603.

Raney, Karen. *Art in Question*. London: Continuum, 2003.

Reinhardt, Kurt F., trans. and ed. *The Dark Night of the Soul*. New York: Unger, 1957.

Rochelle, Gabriel C. "Apophatic Preaching and the Postmodern Mind." *St Vladimir's Theological Quarterly* 50/4 (2006) 397–419.

Rolt, C. E., trans. *Dionysius, the Areopagite: On the Divine Names and Mystical Theology*. London: SPCK, 1920.

Romaine, James, and Linda Stratford, eds. *ReVisioning: Critical Methods of Seeing: Christianity in the History of Art*. Eugene, OR: Cascade, 2014.

Ross, David, ed. *Bill Viola*. New York: Whitney Museum of American Art, 1998.

Rush, Michael. *Video Art*. New York: Thames & Hudson, 2007.

Scharfstein, Ben-Ami. *Ineffability: The Failure of Words in Philosophy and Religion*. Albany: State University of New York Press, 1993.

Scott, David. *Pictorialist Poetics: Poetry and the Visual Arts in Nineteenth-Century France*. Cambridge: Cambridge University Press, 2009.

Sells, Michael. *Mystical Languages of Unsaying*. Chicago: University of Chicago Press, 1994.

Shaw, Philip. *The Sublime*. New Critical Idiom. New York: Routledge, 2006.

Smith, Barry D. *The Indescribable God: Divine Otherness in Christian Theology*. Eugene, OR: Pickwick, 2012

Taylor, Cheryl. "The *Cloud* Texts and Some Aspects of Modern Theory." *Mystics Quarterly* 24/4 (2001) 143–53.

Taylor, Marc C. *Disfiguring: Art, Architecture and Religion*. Chicago: University of Chicago Press, 1992.

Townsend, Chris, ed. *The Art of Bill Viola*. London: Thames & Hudson, 2004.

Turner, Denys. "The Art of Unknowing: Negative Theology in Late Medieval Mysticism." *Modern Theology* 14/4 (1998) 473–88.

————. *The Darkness of God: Negativity in Christian Mysticism*. Cambridge: Cambridge University Press, 1995.

Viola, Bill. *Reasons for Knocking At an Empty House: Writings, 1973–1994*. London: Thames & Hudson, 1995.

Walsh, John, ed. *Bill Viola: The Passions*. Los Angeles: Getty, 2003.

Ward, Graham. *Theology and Contemporary Critical Theory*. New York: St. Martin's, 2000.

Will, Maika J. "Dionysian Neoplatonism and the Theology of the *Cloud* Author—I." *The Downside Review* 110/379 (April 1992) 98–109.

Williams, J. P. *Denying Divinity: Apophasis in the Patristic Christian and Soto Zen Buddhist Traditions*. Oxford: Oxford University Press, 2000.

Žižek, Slavoj. *The Sublime Object of Ideology*. New York: Verso, 1989.

Printed in Great Britain
by Amazon